The Soviet Economy

The Soviet Economy

David A. Dyker

Crosby Lockwood Staples   London

Granada Publishing Limited
First published in Great Britain 1976 by
Crosby Lockwood Staples
Frogmore St Albans Hertfordshire AL2 2NF and
3 Upper James Street London W1R 4BP

Copyright © 1976 by David A. Dyker

ISBN 0 258 96950 4

Printed in Great Britain by
Cox & Wyman Ltd
London, Fakenham and Reading

Preface

My aim in this work has been to give a *brief* account of the Soviet economic system, and to place it in historical and developmental perspective. I make no apologies, therefore, for the selectivity of the treatment. The reader will find only the most perfunctory account of areas of secondary interest, such as internal trade. He may be surprised to find key areas like foreign trade treated in the same cavalier fashion. The argument here was quite simply that, however important the external sector, particularly with a view to the future, it has not played a crucial role in the developmental dynamic of the Soviet system. Even on topics which do receive extended coverage, however, specialists may be surprised at certain omissions. My aim has been to write neither an economic history, nor an account of economic policy, and many empirical details which would have to be treated in works of that nature have not been mentioned because they are not crucial to my central themes. On the other hand, quite minor points have been given what may appear to be disproportionate attention, because they seem to me to throw light on the nature of command systems, and on the nature of the developmental process.

A number of people have provided indispensable help in the preparation of the book. Roger A. Clarke of the University of Glasgow read the whole manuscript, Professor G. M. Heal of the University of Sussex read Chapter 2, and Mary McAuley of the University of Essex Chapter 6. They made many useful criticisms and suggestions, and have helped to excise a number of faults in the original draft. For the faults that remain, and indeed for the book as a whole, I, of course, am wholly responsible. Mrs J. Gibbins of Brighton typed the whole manuscript, Sue Rowland of the University of Sussex drew the maps, and Naomi-Jane Dyker helped with the illustrations. I must also express my thanks to that admirable journal *ABSEES*, which so often provided signposts on obscure points.

I am grateful to Professor V. G. Treml of Duke University for permission to reproduce Table 3, to Dr M. Ellman of the University of Cambridge for permission to reproduce Table 4, to the University of Wisconsin Press for permission to reproduce the passage on page 48, and to the University of North Carolina Press for permission to reproduce the passage on page 151.

D. A. Dyker
University of Sussex
March, 1976

Contents

CHAPTER ONE

Preliminaries

THE HISTORICAL BACKGROUND

It is of primary importance to place the Soviet economic system in proper historical context, and to avoid the danger of using a static approach where a dynamic is appropriate. Unlike the British, American or French systems, the Soviet system did not evolve slowly and organically through pre-industrial and industrial periods. It was developed by politicians and administrators in the space of about six years at a time when the USSR was embarking on a massive, state-directed, industrialization programme. It would be reckless to say that the system was consciously worked out as a solution to a problem of economic backwardness. But it cannot be doubted that in practice Soviet planning has operated as an instrument of development.

The Russian economy on the eve of the First World War was neither wholly undeveloped nor completely stagnant. Considerable industrial centres existed in Petersburg, Moscow, the Donbass/Krivoi Rog area of the Ukraine, and Baku in the Caucasus. Around 9 million people, one-seventeenth of the total population, were employed in industry, commerce, transportation, etc.[1] In terms of scale and technology, the leading Russian industrial establishments like the Putilov works in Petersburg could be ranked in world terms.[2] Early railway development, starting in the 1860s, was followed by a fairly highly integrated policy of heavy-industrial development in the 1890s, under the leadership of the energetic Finance Minister,

Sergei Witte.[3] Despite setbacks around the turn of the century – worldwide depression was soon followed by the disastrous Russo-Japanese War – the economy sustained respectable average annual rates of growth right up to 1913. Between 1899 and 1913 production of coal grew by 47 per cent and that of pig iron by 72 per cent, while output of iron and steel grew from 2·5 to 4·1 million tons.[4] Even agriculture, while retaining its basic characteristics – small-scale, peasant and over-manned – showed increases in production. Grain output grew by 46 per cent between 1899 and 1913.[5] The policies of Peter Stolypin, Prime Minister from 1907 to 1911, helped to break down a number of legal impediments to the development of modern, individual farming.[6] But the economy remained at an early stage of development, as was shown with brutal clarity when it came into collision with the German military-industrial establishment in the course of the First World War.

The economic situation presenting itself in 1921, after seven years of war, revolution and counter-revolution, was, however, much less favourable than it had been in 1913. The policies of War Communism (1918–21) were marked by wholesale nationalization, compulsory procurement amounting to confiscation of agricultural products, and a high degree of centralization. The relative importance of ideological and practical considerations during this period remains the subject of controversy. Some Bolshevik leaders seem to have envisaged a direct transition to Full Communism in its strict Marxian sense, and Lenin himself was at least ambivalent on this point. On the other hand, militarization of economic administration no doubt aided rapid mobilization of resources in a desperate military situation. What is certainly the case is that total emphasis on the short run and disregard for investment needs, combined with the sheer physical destruction of those terrible years, eventually produced a situation of near-collapse.[7] In 1920 gross industrial production in large-scale industry was only 14·4 per cent of its 1913 level.[8] Cement production was down to 1 per cent of its prewar level, reflecting the virtual cessation of investment during the years of upheaval.[9]

It was against this background that the policies of NEP (New Economic Policy) were formulated. Small-scale industry and trade were denationalized, large-scale industry decentralized, and arbitrary agricultural procurements replaced by free trade in agricultural products, tempered by taxation. Whether NEP was from its inception seen as merely a temporary retreat, or was meant to indicate the path of long-term Soviet development, remains another controversial issue. Certainly the 1920s were essentially years of recovery. Industrial production regained its 1913 level in 1927, while agricultural production achieved the same landmark in 1925.[10] This essentially short-term issue of recovery did, indeed, considerably influence the views and theories of Soviet writers on long-term development policy from this period. In particular, feelings that large-scale investment in heavy industry would be a necessary condition for rapid industrial growth were reinforced by a consciousness that capital use during the War Communism period meant a 'hump' in capital replacement needs, i.e. a situation of having to 'run faster to stay in the same place'.[11] When the final decision to embark on a crash industrialization programme was taken it was, of course, taken by Stalin, very much a politician and organization man, not by the intellectuals who debated so brilliantly in that first postwar decade. Crash industrialization was, furthermore, intimately tied in with the decision to impose collectivization on the private peasantry – still the majority of the population – and it has been plausibly argued that this latter decision was the culmination of a series of errors and policy bungles.[12] One should certainly not look for too much logic and foresight in the momentous decisions of 1928–32. With the benefit of hindsight, however, we can discern a strategy of development based fundamentally on industry, very concerned with rapid growth, bent on self-sufficiency,[13] and hence bound to place first priority on the development of producer goods industries as a precondition for the maintenance of a high investment rate. In the absence of foreign investment, which was not forthcoming whether the Soviet authorities wanted it or not, an internal source of finance had to be found for this operation. The industrial sector was by definition small and weak. The agricultural sector, through sheer size if not through high productivity, could be made to yield some surplus. So it was that collectivization, rather than being a policy for agriculture, turned out to be a policy for industry. The collective farm became an 'instrument of collection, rather than an instrument of collective work'.[14] Emphasis was placed almost exclusively on the

[3]

procurement of agricultural products for the urban sector, the rural standard of living was forced down to, and sometimes even below, bare subsistence level. Investment flows into agriculture were minimal.[15] Thus, even at the simplest two-sector level, the Soviet strategy for development was essentially one of imbalance.

PRINCIPAL GEOGRAPHICAL FEATURES OF THE SOVIET UNION

The Soviet Union is a huge country. Its total land area is 8,700,000 square miles, as compared with 94,205 for the UK, 2,566,000 for the USA, and 3,750,000 for China. This may seem an obvious enough point, but it is crucial to emphasize its great importance for the Soviet economy – indeed, it makes the Soviet economy, in at least one important respect which has nothing to do with system, unique. The whole field of transport and locational economics is so much more important for the Soviet than for any other economy in the world. In practice, furthermore, specific features of the Soviet area make distance even more crucial than it would be anyway. A glance at Maps 1 and 2 will indicate an unfortunate tendency for major raw material deposits and power resources to be located well away from the principal centres of population. There are exceptions to this, notably the Donbass/Krivoi Rog area of the Ukraine. But in general, the big deposits of natural resources tend to be found to the east and north, while the old settled areas to the south and west, where the weather is less inclement, are relatively poorly endowed. To make matters worse, different types of resources, complementary in production, are often found far away from each other, as can be seen from Map 2. Coal and ferrous ore deposits are rarely found together – again the outstanding exception is the Donbass/Krivoi Rog region. In general power resources are most abundant in Siberia and Central Asia, while ore deposits are concentrated in the Urals, the north-west, and the Caucasus.

It is also very important to bear in mind how far north the Soviet Union lies. Leningrad is on roughly the same latitude as Anchorage in Alaska, and even Odessa, on the Black Sea, is only slightly farther south than Quebec. As can be seen from Map 2, the percentage of the total Soviet area that is permanently

[4]

frozen below a certain depth is large, and this creates problems, not only for agriculture but also for construction.

THE FUNDAMENTAL CHARACTERISTICS OF THE COMMAND ECONOMY

The Soviet economy is commonly described as a centrally planned economy. Less commonly, the term command economy is used.[16] These descriptions are, in fact, usually taken to be synonymous. Yet a moment's thought shows that they lay emphasis on quite different things. Is one misleading, or indeed downright wrong? Or are they equally illuminating, in diverse but partial ways?

There can be no doubt that the Soviet economy is subject to a very high degree of central control. There is virtually no freedom of price-fixing for producing units in the USSR, except with respect to a small, though important, proportion of agricultural produce which is sold direct to the public through special markets. Contractual relationships are determined from above, except in those same agricultural markets and in the labour and retail goods markets. Specific production tasks for a large number of commodity groups are worked out by one or other of the central planning agencies. There can be little doubt then that the contemporary Soviet economy is, in an obvious and important sense, centralized, perhaps overcentralized. But it can be argued, paradoxically, that the principal problems of the Soviet economy flow from the fact that it is not centralized enough. Factories produce low-quality goods because the central authorities do not, or cannot, specify in sufficient detail the precise grades required, or are unable effectively to monitor whether established standards have been met. The same factories may get away with violation of reasonable cost constraints for the same reasons. But clearly the problem cannot be insufficient degree of centralization per se. After all, in more or less decentralized capitalist economies quality considerations and cost constraints are more or less observed. Our attention is thus drawn to the basis on which any given degree of centralization or decentralization takes effect at the level of actual production. In the Soviet case our attention is drawn to the command principle.

The nexus of economic activity in a capitalist economy, and

[5]

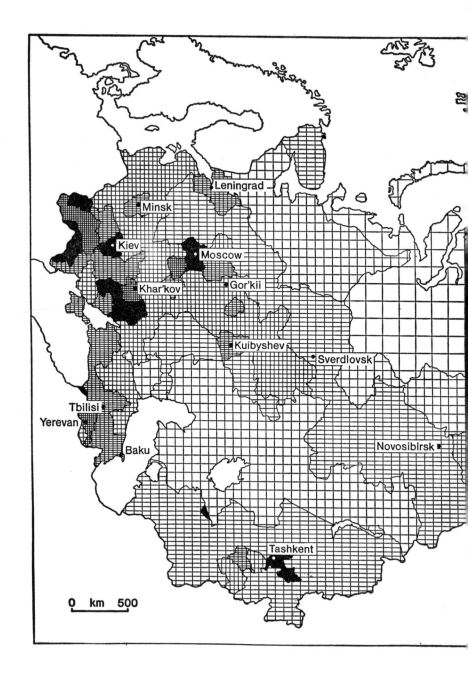

Map 1 Population density by administrative area

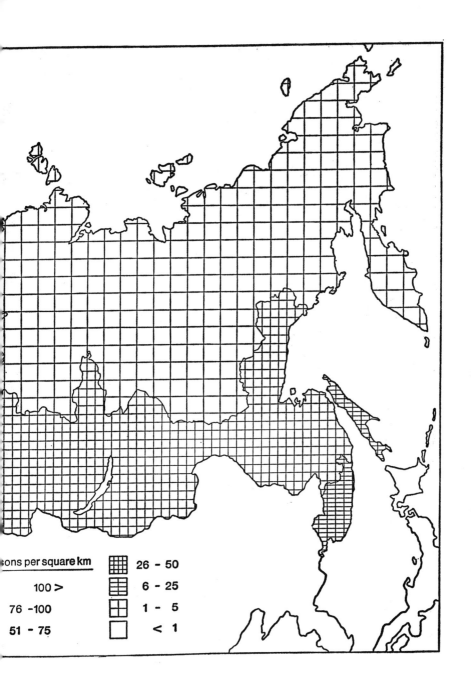

ons per **square km**

	100 >
76 -100	
51 - 75	

⊞	26 - 50
⊞	6 - 25
⊞	1 - 5
☐	< 1

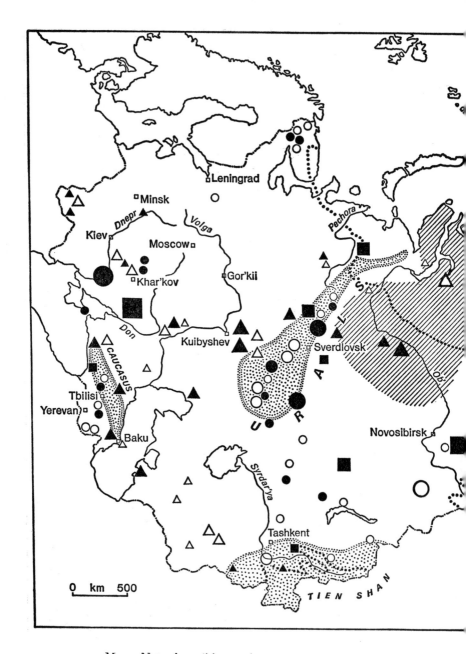

Map 2 Natural conditions and resources
   Note: No attempt has been made to give systematic coverage of total resource endowment, as
   opposed to actual extraction. The Tyumen[1] oil-
   field and Tungus and Lena coalfields are marked
   because of their quite unique potential importance.

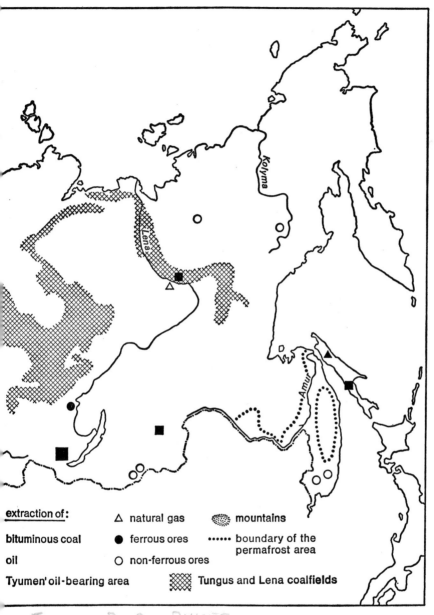

extraction of:

bituminous coal

oil

Tyumen' oil-bearing area

△ natural gas

● ferrous ores

○ non-ferrous ores

🌑 mountains

•••••• boundary of the permafrost area

▨ **Tungus and Lena coalfields**

FROM - D. A. DYKER.
" THE SOVIET ECONOMY"

(pub Crosby, Lockwood Staples 1976)

indeed in some kinds of socialist economy, is the market. In a Soviet-type economy the nexus of economic activity is the instruction passed from hierarchical superior to hierarchical inferior. In a capitalist economy managements make profits, gain prestige, achieve growth, by selling to potential buyers. In a Soviet-type economy managements may not be particularly interested in profits or growth as such – of this more later – but can maximize personal emoluments and gain prestige through the fulfilment of set tasks.

As everyone knows the market does not always operate in a particularly efficient way in a capitalist economy. Customers do not always receive precisely what they want, they may be misled into buying something they do not, in the light of subsequent reflection, really need, and they may have to buy at prices which do not correspond to actual scarcities. The extent to which the capitalist economy is subject to such distortions is, of course, the subject of some controversy. Distortions in the command-fulfilment process in the Soviet-type economy are more obvious, and there is little controversy about their form and quantitative importance, even between Western and Soviet economists. What is important is to understand fully the fundamental nature of these distortions. Even where the planners are in possession of more or less adequate information, they are faced with the problem of expressing the planning instruction in terms of some indicator or other. If we consider the kinds of simple, non-synthetic indicators which the Soviets have used in the past – gross output, net output, assortment, cost reduction, etc. – we note that each one of them concentrates exclusive attention on just one aspect of the production process. Unless one is prepared to visualize a system where a large number of such indicators is used as the basis for an incentive system carefully weighted to produce a pattern corresponding to priorities as to, for example, the relative importance of cost and quality considerations – and this would involve insuperable problems of principle and practice – then simple indicators will tend to induce some kind of one-sidedness in production decision-making. Discussion of attempts to cope with this problem through the development of complex, synthetic indicators will take up a large part of the following. What is important at the present juncture is to note that it is the presence of the command principle which creates the problem in the first place, not the degree of centralization or decentralization. For this reason it is more helpful to use the term command to characterize Soviet-type economies, while bearing in mind the enormous significance of the level of centralization in any organizational system. In this way we emphasize the importance of means of plan implementation, as distinct from plan construction.

BASIC ADMINISTRATIVE STRUCTURE

The structure which evolved in the industrial and urban services sectors in the early 1930s was based on a three-tier hierarchy. At the top was *Gosplan*, and other central planning agencies. Then came the intermediate stage – the ministry. Initially there were only three industrial ministries – heavy, light and timber – but their number soon grew, and by 1939 stood at twenty. Major sub-divisions of ministries were called *glavki* (singular *glavk*), and in times of proliferation of the number of ministries, *glavki* were often promoted to ministerial status. This hierarchy has remained basically the same to the present day, though the precise relationships between the different levels have been modified. From 1957 to 1965 the ministries/*glavki* were replaced by a system of *sovnarkhozy* – regional economic councils. We shall be discussing the significance of this reform later – we mention it here merely to avoid possible confusion in supplementary reading. We shall in any case use the term intermediate body as a general term for ministry, *glavk* and *sovnarkhoz*.

Another potential source of confusion lies in the occasional, though increasingly frequent, intervention of a fourth tier between the intermediate and enterprise level. In the past, enterprises have sometimes been grouped together into trusts (*tresti*, singular *trest*), combines (*kombinaty*, singular *kombinat*), firms (*firmy*, singular *firma*) and associations (*ob''edineniya* – singular *ob''edinenie*). As we shall see later, the association has come into particular prominence since 1973. Under these various arrangements enterprises have sometimes retained autonomy, sometimes not. Sometimes associations and combines have attained virtual *glavk* status. The different names are, indeed, often very little indication of the exact nature of the organization, and we must just accept this as a complex and somewhat confusing phenomenon. One point that is worth noting – in the building industry almost all enterprises are organized into trusts, and the trust can for practical purposes be considered the primary producing unit in this sector.

In agriculture the predominant form of organization, the *kolkhoz* (collective farm), is rather different. It is nominally an autonomous, self-governing unit with an elected chairman. In practice the absence of the status of state enterprise has meant simply that the state has not taken responsibility for even the short-term welfare of the organization or its members, rather than that it has refrained from interfering in internal *kolkhoz* affairs. *Kolkhozy* have been subject to regular and large-scale compulsory procurements, and over most of the post-1928 period these have been at very low prices, while capital equipment, free to state enterprises up to 1965, has been charged to collective farms at relatively high prices. *Kolkhozniki* (collective farm workers – singular *kolkhoznik*) have, until very recently, received as payment only a share of the residual left after all other obligations had been met.

In the early days, this residual was often quite inadequate to sustain life. It is against this background that we can note one of the reasons why the private plot has been so important. *Kolkhozniki* have been permitted to cultivate or use as pasture small areas of land on their own account, with the right to sell the produce thereof freely, and at the price the market would bear, short of infringing the anti-speculation laws.[17] The private plot has been a crucial source of subsistence to the *kolkhoznik*, and has provided important additional cash flows.

In addition to *kolkhozy* there are *sovkhozy* (state farms). These are state enterprises, and operate in a way not fundamentally different from industrial enterprises. *Sovkhoz* workers are, however, permitted to have private plots. The *sovkhoz* sector has increased considerably in relative importance since the 1950s, with the conversion of some *kolkhozy* and the implementation of the Virgin Lands scheme, which was based exclusively on the *sovkhoz* form of organization. Before leaving agriculture it is worth noting that many non-agricultural rural and suburban workers exercise the right to cultivate private plots.[18]

Foreign trade is organized in a special way. Specialized associations hold a monopoly for import and export, or both, within a particular commodity group. Industrial and agricultural enterprises have no direct involvement in foreign trade at all. These arrangements reflect a degree of detailed, direct central control exercised in the external sector, distinguishing it from most sectors of the internal economy, though not perhaps from the top-priority defence and space-research sectors.

Then we have the design organizations (*proektnye organizatsii*), which work out the details of investment projects approved at central or intermediate level. There are many different types of these, and they may be subordinate to intermediate bodies, or local authorities, or even directly to the central authorities. Closely related to the design organizations are the various applied research institutes. At least until very recently, these R & D organizations have worked largely outside the framework of production administration.

In addition to the major forms of economic administration, various 'odd bods' can be found. Consumer co-operatives are co-operatives only in name. For all practical purposes they are nothing more than rural branches of the state retail network. Private artisans survive in sectors such as shoe-repairing, subject to heavy rates of taxation.

FISCAL AND MONETARY INSTITUTIONS

It goes without saying that this kind of institution, crucially important in a market system, fulfils only a secondary role in the command economy. But the command principle is not universally enforced in the Soviet Union, so that a number of important functions are fulfilled by these 'traditional' means of state control. Turnover tax has played an important part in bringing the Soviet price structure into line with demand conditions in consumer goods markets. Income tax survives, though it hardly seems necessary as a means of redistribution in a system where production and wage-rates are under such a high degree of central control. Direct taxation has, however, been an important means of extracting funds from the *kolkhoz* sector, and of discouraging private artisan activity. The so-called bachelor's tax may furnish some incentive to procreation within the institution of matrimony. Monetary control is of secondary importance as far as aggregate demand is concerned – though it does form a possible, though not always very effective, long-stop against repressed-inflationary pressures created by illegal or semi-legal payments and plan shortfalls. Much more important is the inspection role played by the banks, to which we shall direct our attention in the next section. The general importance of the financial sector has increased considerably since 1965, with the introduction of profit as a major plan indicator, and increased emphasis placed on inter-organization monetary flows.

INSPECTION BODIES

A number of disparate organizations are concerned with what the Russians call *kontrol*[1] – attempting to ensure that central plan directives are fulfilled in the spirit in which they were intended, and to restrain the proliferation of the distortive tendencies already briefly mentioned. The local echelons of the Communist Party play a part in this, though they are subject to many pressures which make it difficult for them to play the part properly, as we shall see later. The Committee of People's Control, formerly the Central Control Commission, employs inspectors who have access to files and the right of questioning. *Gosbank* (State Bank) controls the working capital of most enterprises, and furnishes invest-ment loans to the *kolkhoz* sector of agriculture. *Stroibank* (Con-struction Bank) was created in 1959 as a successor to specialized industrial, agricultural, etc. banks, and handles the finance of the bulk of fixed investment in the state sector, including the state farm sector. These arrangements give *Gosbank* and *Stroibank* considerable scope for the monitoring of the investment process. How effectively they use this scope we shall see in a later chapter.

SOME BASIC STATISTICS AND STATISTICAL PROBLEMS

Much has been written about the quantitative evaluation of Soviet economic performance and the structure of the Soviet economy, not all of it in a particularly objective way. The Soviet authorities themselves have placed such emphasis on growth, and framed their claims to economic success so much in terms of growth, that it is perhaps inevitable that growth rates should become the centre of substantive controversy. Again, the strategic interest in the fundamental proportions of the economy – particularly, obviously, the percentage of national income devoted to defence – has introduced an element of excitement into the normally pedestrian field of structural analysis. But there are some fundamental theoretical problems seriously affecting statistical analysis of the Soviet economy, and it is to those that we turn first.

Most fundamentally of all, there is the index-number problem. In any economy undergoing a process of rapid growth and structural change, the difference between a *Paasche* (end-year price weights) estimate and a *Laspeyres* (starting-year price weights) is enormous. One well-known Western estimate of the Soviet growth rate between 1928 and 1937, i.e. in the period of fundamental transformation, comes up with a figure of 4·8 per cent with a *Paasche* index and 11·9 per cent with a *Laspeyres*![19] It is quite common for so-called 'rolling indices' to be used to try to cope with this problem. With this method a composite index is built up by calculating, say, 1928 and 1929 national income in 1929 prices, then 1929 and 1930 national income in 1930 prices, and so on. It must, however, be recognized that the basic problem is one of trying to compare like with unlike. The difference between the Soviet economy of 1928 and the Soviet economy of 1937 is the difference between an essentially undeveloped economy and an industrial, though not a mature industrial, economy. No degree of statistical sophistication can get round this basic chalk/cheese problem. We have to accept that attempts at precision in this kind of calculation are fundamentally spurious.

In practical terms, however, the problem of prices is much more general than that. Meaningful aggregation of economic data must be based on an approximation to scarcity prices. No actual price system gives anything but a fairly crude approximation, but there are special difficulties in the Soviet case. Soviet price planners have never made any attempt to orientate their work to scarcity considerations. A mark-up approach has been, and remains, prevalent. This is partly due to ideological prejudice – the Marxian labour theory of value remains the officially endorsed basis for price-setting. But in any case the existing level of computer technology would not permit the calculation of scarcity prices for the hundreds of thousands of commodity groups for which prices are set centrally, even if the necessary information for the calculations were available, which it is not. Things, however, have often been worse even than this general picture suggests. So vast is the number of prices to be fixed that serious anomalies, even by the standards of official practice, have often been present, though the 1967 price reform reduced, at least temporarily, the incidence of this sort of thing.[20] Other deviations from the standard mark-up have reflected official policy. Air transport charges have been deliberately kept down, as have coal prices and rail transport charges across Siberia, though the effect of the 1967 reform has been to limit the scope for such practices.

The 1965 industrial planning reform introduced for the first time a charge on capital. The charge has, however, been set at a level – usually 6 per cent – which has been argued by Soviet economists to be much too low adequately to reflect real scarcity conditions.[21] No proper system of land rent has ever existed in the Soviet Union, though the subject has been under much discussion of late.[22] The rather crude system of zoned procurement prices does, in fact, represent some kind of rent-substitute for agriculture, while the 1967 reform introduced a form of rent payment for extractive industries. Contemporary pricing practice does not, then, ignore the valuation of non-labour factors of production completely. But the incidence of interest and rent payments remains uneven and/or too low, and this maintains major and systematic elements of distortion in the Soviet price system.

There is another problem also related to official Marxist doctrine which affects aggregated indices, though not prices *per se*. All Soviet national income figures ignore the contribution of so-called 'non-productive' sectors, i.e. services, non-business passenger transport, etc. In addition, the Soviet concept of 'gross social product' involves a great deal of double-counting. It should be noted, however, that there is no *a priori* reason why these peculiarities should affect estimates of rates of growth, as opposed to estimates of absolute figures.

When all this is added up it becomes clear that any attempt to measure any economic magnitude for the Soviet Union is fraught with difficulties, even if no index-number problem is involved.

The temptation, then, is to turn to physical indicators. Quite apart from the fact that these cannot be properly aggregated in their raw form, however, there are still problems in connection with the reliability of Soviet reporting.

Important pieces of information are sometimes suppressed by the central authorities. No production figures, for example, have ever been published for non-ferrous metallurgy. Definitions are sometimes grossly misleading in formulation. Thus it is commonly suspected that the innocuous-sounding 'medium-machine building' sector in fact concentrates on the production of crucial strategic goods.[23] There is, however, no evidence that the official Soviet statisticians habitually 'fiddle' figures as such, though there may have been one or two outstanding examples.[24] This is not to say, of course, that there is no tendency to choose the index that will produce the figure reflecting best on the Soviet Union. But the big problem, as far as veracity in reporting is concerned, is with the reporting of primary and intermediate organizations to the centre. The managing cadres of these organizations know very well that the plans they will be set are to a great extent a function of the information they supply. So one primary result of the gearing of the system to plan fulfilment is a tendency for lower-level organizations to over-indent for supplies and underestimate capital capacity. The central planners do, of course, know perfectly well that this sort of thing goes on, and attempt to make allowances for it in ways which we will be discussing in the next chapter. In the present context, however, we must simply note that in extreme cases this tendency may affect information, not just on production capabilities, but on production itself. Output may be 'borrowed' from one production period to another,[25] and cases of outright falsification of production figures do come to light from time to time. In Tadzhikistan in 1961, for example, the top Communist Party cadres were almost completely cleaned out for alleged falsification of agricultural production figures.[26] We must, then, be prepared for an element of distortion in Soviet statistics even where problems of prices and price indices are avoided, and this is particularly difficult to trace in particular instances because it originates at the grass-roots level.

When all is said and done, however, it is possible to state with some confidence that 'despite some justifiable scepticism about certain Soviet data ... the published physical output series and many other figures must be taken seriously'.[27] Aggregated indices remain something of a problem. For this reason I have brought together some of the principal estimates of Soviet growth rates in Table 1, as an indication of orders of magnitude and the scope of the problem. The official Soviet and Nutter estimates can be taken as, respectively, the high and low limiting cases.

TABLE I

Estimates of Soviet Growth Rates

National Income	Official Soviet	Bergson	Cohn
1928–37	16·3	5·0–5·5	4·8–11·9
1950–55	11·4	7·5–7·6	6·9
1955–58	10·2		7·4
1958–61	7·3		5·4
1961–65	8·5		5·2
1965–68	7·6		
1968–72	5·8		

Industrial Production	Official Soviet	Nutter	Greenslade
1928–37	16·1	12·1	
1950–55	13·1	9·6	9·7–10·7
1955–58	10·3	7·1	
1955–60	10·4		8·8–9·3
1960–65	8·6		6·5–7·0
1965–68	8·9		5·7–6·8
1968–72	7·4		
1970–72	7·1		5·6

SOURCES
Various editions of *Narodnoe Khozyaistvo SSSR*, Moscow.
A. Bergson, *The Real National Income of Soviet Russia since 1928*, Harvard University Press, Cambridge, Mass., 1961, pp. 219 and 222.
S. H. Cohn, 'Analysis of the Soviet growth model', in ed. M. Bornstein and D. R. Fusfeld, *The Soviet Economy – a Book of Readings*, 3rd ed., Irwin, Homewood, Illinois, 1970, p. 302.
G. W. Nutter, *Growth of Industrial Production in the Soviet Union*, NBER and Princeton University Press, Princeton, 1962, p. 287.
R. V. Greenslade, 'Industrial production statistics in the USSR', in ed. V. G. Treml and J. P. Hardt, *Soviet Economic Statistics*, Duke University Press, Durham, N. Carolina, 1972, p. 168.
R. V. Greenslade and W. E. Robertson, 'Industrial production in the USSR', in US Congress, Joint Economic Committee, *Soviet Economic Prospects for the Seventies*, US Government Printing Office, Washington DC, 1973, p. 278.

[18]

Table ? Principal Macro-economic Proportions of the Soviet Economy (in percentages)

	Personal Consumption (Becker)	Collective Consumption, Science and Administration (Becker)	Net Fixed Capital Investment (Becker)	Net Fixed Capital Investment (Kaplan)	Increment of Working Capital and Reserves (Becker)	Total	
1937				12.4		100	(Gross National Product)
1948				14.0–14.5		100	
1950	69.2	6.9	13.1		10.8	100	(Net Material Product)
1955	68.0	6.3	14.0		11.7	100	
1958	66.3	6.4	17.2		10.1	100	
1961	64.0	7.6	16.8		11.7	100	
1965	65.6	8.1	14.6		11.7	100	
1968	65.0	8.3	13.9		12.9	100	

	Private Consumption (Cohn)	Communal Consumption (Cohn)	Total Gross Investment Fixed and Inventory (Cohn)	Defence (Cohn)	Other (Cohn)	Total	
1928	64.7	5.1	25.0	2.5	2.7	100	(Gross National Product)
1937	52.5	10.5	25.9	7.9	3.2	100	
1940	51.0	9.9	19.2	16.1	3.8	100	
1950	53.6–54.7	5.4–5.5	23.4–23.9	10.8–12.6	5.0–5.1	100	
1955	54.5	5.3	25.1	12.3	2.8	100	
1965	50.7–51.3	6.5–6.6	30.5–30.8	9.1–10.1	2.2	100	
1969	50.7–50.9	7.1	29.4–29.5	10.1–10.4	2.4	100	

SOURCES

A. S. Becker, 'National Income accounting in the USSR', in eds. V. G. Treml and J. P. Hardt, Soviet Economic Statistics, Duke University Press, Durham, North Carolina, 1972, p. 98.

N. M. Kaplan, 'Capital formation and allocation' in ed. A. Bergson, Soviet Economic Growth, Row, Peterson, Evanston, Illinois, and New York, 1953, p. 47.

S. H. Cohn, 'Analysis of the Soviet growth model' in eds. M. Bornstein and D. R. Fusfeld, The Soviet Economy – a Book of Readings, 3rd ed., Irwin, Homewood, Illinois, 1970, p. 310.

S. H. Cohn, 'Economic burden of defense expenditures', in Soviet Economic Prospects for the Seventies, US Government Printing Office, Washington DC, 1973, p. 160.

TABLE 3 (see Note opposite)

18-Sector Input–Output Matrix of the Soviet Economy for 1966 (000s of roubles)
Outputs

	Inputs	1	2	3	4	5
1	Metals	8188157	82822	18691	6907144	2355000
2	Fuels	1908076	3196273	2656182	513576	327100
3	Power	781500	559450	11456	728790	352900
4	Engineering (published)	571671	253544	76272	8526658	1033700
5	Engineering (other)	96321	42327	23118	2075550	1355100
6	Chemicals (published)	369894	242534	23371	1813489	334700
7	Synthetic rubber	200	100	0	55400	0
8	Wood and paper	113711	384101	4384	613042	265900
9	Construction materials	33425	31496	3295	95715	43200
10	Glass	9785	3064	1176	177898	81300
11	Industry not elsewhere classified	56143	31063	18646	190057	42900
12	Textiles	172621	74262	9249	548640	84600
13	Food	46328	19805	5425	121808	27200
	All industry	12347832	4920841	2851265	22367767	6303600
14	Construction	0	0	0	0	0
15	Agriculture and forestry	1988	992	0	2542	0
16	Transport and communications	1880082	4475021	4119	1897332	176100
17	Trade and distribution	517596	1007076	400	658870	230700
18	Other branches	319713	174	790	71374	16200
	Total purchases	15067211	10404104	2856574	24997885	6726600
	Depreciation	1577687	1687028	1159410	1859234	455202
	National income	7163662	6988968	3511316	21839381	3818198
	Total outlay	23808560	19080100	7527300	48696500	11000000

	6	7	8	9	10	11	12	13
1	559938	19100	188287	697079	46964	777800	46433	238769
2	422870	96800	356235	644569	67465	267600	110786	622100
3	664855	69300	220570	386931	28913	254300	249499	224564
4	169505	3400	383908	262380	36711	291900	235527	361666
5	40701	0	26452	43372	9036	44100	41239	39041
6	3045160	247600	381031	162168	85981	1176100	1340240	180445
7	928300	900	3300	700	0	0	111900	100
8	405991	107600	4559387	180861	53244	1867800	171908	627454
9	18908	100	27860	1937386	18300	60200	12315	45809
10	74497	400	100947	46381	37812	15600	8110	115470
11	135322	0	54277	119004	3852	212000	272630	224644
12	587230	2200	387119	91614	14562	439400	26958593	528783
13	580341	81600	56816	60422	1940	1408400	701362	22073346
		7633618	629000	674189	4632867	404780	6815200	30260542	25282191
14	0	0	0	0	0	0	0	0
15	35055	0	203452	1192	237	395179	5441498	31188522
16	953485	70700	2262582	3861450	133227	180621	433220	1454801
17	376466	11700	583438	135620	71842	808775	1679494	6986523
18	7854	0	46555	22721	2253	107468	25390	36211
	9006478	711400	9842216	8653850	612339	8307243	37840144	64948248
	697384	38364	861969	781680	55515	927500	440358	958669
	5384438	163236	5041915	4064470	1084146	2570697	19049498	23820083
	15088300	913000	15746100	13500000	1752000	11805440	57330000	89727000

	AI	14	15	16	17	18	Total Final Demand	Total Domestic Output
1	20126184	2039035	51026	102733	22175	1692	1465715	23808560
2	11189632	678623	1510105	1765962	214793	6076	3714909	19080100
3	4533028	297565	186770	457683	154041	9165	1889048	7527300
4	12206842	3477587	1745304	663231	196096	8031	30399409	48696500
5	3836357	118935	0	107522	16485	1623	6919078	11000000
6	9402713	669622	1265285	522496	99794	27062	3101328	15088300
7	1100900	0	0	0	0	0	-187900	913000
8	9355383	2997601	259540	167187	380772	172187	2413430	15746100
9	2328009	9656129	184420	35004	59961	1038	1235439	13500000
10	672440	501108	22767	7499	66098	282	481806	1752000
11	1360538	1046565	580438	84178	263215	208077	8262429	11805440
12	29898873	575385	295723	152567	227809	49865	26129778	57330000
13	25184793	148115	898625	14099	341296	241	63139831	89727000
	131195692	22206270	7000003	4080161	2042535	485339	148964300	315974300
14	0	0	0	0	0	0	0	0
15	37270657	30500	17595384	6155	81404	15900	28786500	43360000
16	17782740	47693	924749	53577	144145	47096	0	19000000
17	13068500	0	2816800	0	0	264700	0	16150000
18	656703	529500	58200		92978	12619	1890000	3240000
	199974292	22813963	28395136	4139893	2361062	825654	223000800	481510800
	11500000	1446000	4791400	2660000	1226000	35000	10000000	31658400
	104500008	19100037	50599964	12200107	12562938	2379346		
	315974300	43360000	83786500	19000000	16150000	3240000		

NOTE TO TABLE 3
The contribution of a given sector to the production of other sectors can be found by reading along the row for that sector. The origin of the inputs of a given sector can be found by reading down the column for that sector. Total levels of gross output for each sector can be read from the total outlay row or total domestic output column. For value added read the National income row.

SOURCE
V. G. Treml, et al., The Structure of the Soviet Economy, Praeger, New York, Washington and London, 1972, pp. 402–404.

As far as structure of the economy is concerned, there is less controversy, except with respect to the proportions of national income devoted to defence. Table 2 contains a Western collation of official Soviet figures, ignoring defence as such, a Western recalculation including an estimate for defence, plus figures on fixed investment for some early years. Table 3, a fairly highly aggregated input–output matrix, is a Western reconstruction of Soviet material, and should give some idea of inter-sectoral relationships in the economy.

With this broad outline of the shape and structure of the Soviet economy and economic system we are ready to pass on to a more detailed consideration of the functioning of the system of planning and management. Firstly, we must look more closely at how plans are actually constructed in the Soviet system.

NOTES

1. M. Florinsky, *Russia: a History and an Interpretation*, Macmillan, New York, 1953, Vol. II, p. 1232, quoting S. O. Zagorsky, *State Control of Industry in Russia during the War*, Yale University Press, New Haven, 1928, p. 13.
2. See P. I. Lyashchenko, *Istoriya Narodnogo Khozyaistva*, Gospolizdat, Moscow, 1950, Vol. II, Chap. XI.
3. See T. Von Laue, *Sergei Witte and the Industrialization of Russia*, Columbia University Press, New York, 1963.
4. Lyashchenko, *op. cit.*, p. 395.
5. Ibid.
6. See Florinsky, *op. cit.*, pp. 1214–1224.
7. See M. Dobb, *Soviet Economic Development since 1917*, 6th ed., Routledge, London, 1966, Chap. 5.
8. Lyashchenko, *Istoriya Narodnogo Khozyaistva*, Vol. III, p. 77.
9. Dobb, *op. cit.*, p. 149.
10. Ed. I. A. Gladkov, *Sovetskoe Narodnoe Khozyaistvo v 1921–*

1925 gg. Izdatel'stvo Akademii Nauk SSSR, Moscow, 1960, p. 176.

11. See Ye. Preobrazhenskii, *Novaya Ekonomika*, translated by B. Pearce, *The New Economics*, Clarendon Press, Oxford, 1964.
12. See M. Lewin, 'The immediate background to collectivization', in *Soviet Studies*, October, 1965.
13. In the sense of independence from import of goods, not of import of technology.
14. J. F. Karcz, 'Soviet agriculture: a balance sheet', in ed. V. G. Treml, *The Development of the Soviet Economy: Plan and Performance*, Praeger, New York, Washington and London, 1968, p. 124.
15. See ibid.; E. Strauss, *Soviet Agriculture in Perspective*, Allen & Unwin, London, 1969, Chap. VI; A. Nove, *An Economic History of the USSR*, Penguin, Harmondsworth, 1969, Chap. 7 and pp. 238-244.
16. M. J. Ellman, in his *Planning Problems in the USSR*, Cambridge University Press, Cambridge 1973, uses the term 'administrative economy'.
17. Only those actually involved in production are permitted to sell. There are other restrictions; children, for instance, are forbidden to sell. Newspaper reports, e.g. 'Spekulyanta – za vorota rynka!' in *Kommunist Tadzhikistana*, 24 October 1972, p. 3, allege widespread incidence of speculation and profiteering, and blame 'lack of organization of markets'. Rumours prevalent in 1970 that unofficial price ceilings had been introduced in *kolkhoz* markets were implicitly denied in a reply to a reader's letter in *Ekonomicheskaya Gazeta*, 1/71, p. 16.
18. A. Isaev, 'Ogorod v rabochem prigorode', in *Trud*, 28 April 1973, p. 2.
19. See Table 1.
20. For a discussion of the reform see G. E. Schroeder, 'The 1966-67 Soviet industrial price reform: a study in complications', in *Soviet Studies*, April 1969.
21. See L. Vaag, 'Effektivnost', interesovannost'', in *Ekonomicheskaya Gazeta*, 20 October 1965, pp. 8-9; V. A. Trapeznikov, '"Glagoli" upravleniya: znaet – mozhet – khochet – uspevaet', in *Literaturnaya Gazeta*, 12 May 1970, p. 10.
22. See, for example, N. Federenko, 'Ob ekonomicheskoi otsenke

prirodnykh resursov', in *Voprosy Ekonomiki*, 3/68; V. Pav-
lenko, 'O edinykh metodikakh', in *Ekonomicheskaya Gazeta*,
46/70, p. 7; A. E. Probst, *Voprosy Razmeshcheniya Sotsialisticheskoi Promyshlennosti*, Moscow, 1971, p. 158.
23. See M. Fainsod, *How Russia is Ruled*, revised edition, Harvard
University Press, Cambridge, Mass., 1963, p. 399.
24. See A. Nove, 'Same thoughts while reading the Soviet press',
in *Soviet Studies*, July 1965, and 'Statistical puzzles continue',
in *Soviet Studies*, July 1966.
25. It is worth noting that exactly the same sort of thing goes on
on the shop floor, under piecework conditions, in this
country. See T. Lupton, 'On the shop floor: output and
earnings', in ed. T. Lupton, *Payment Systems*, Penguin,
Harmondsworth, 1972.
26. See Report of VII Plenum CCCP Tadzhikistan, in *Kommunist
Tadzhikistana*, 14 April 1961, pp. 1–2; V. Bulargin, 'Krepit¹
sotsialisticheskuyu zakonnost¹', in *Kommunist Tadzhikistana*,
17 December 1961, p. 2.
27. A. Nove, *The Soviet Economy*, 3rd ed., Allen & Unwin,
London, 1968, p. 354.

CHAPTER TWO

Plan Construction

The process of plan construction falls into three main parts:

1. The gathering of information.
2. The attempt to achieve internal consistency.
3. The allocation of resources.

We have already seen, in Chapter One, some of the problems which the Soviet planners face as far as the gathering of information is concerned. Lower-level organizations 'lay the fat on' and the central planners cut it off. But the central planners can only cut off the fat in a very approximate way. A clever manager is the one who manages to keep some fat. An absolutely honest manager will find himself in an impossible situation because putative fat has been cut off. There are, however, informational problems beyond those created by undesirable managerial practices. With the immense scale of information flows inherent in a high degree of centralization, the problem of storing data in a properly organized and retrievable way is immense. Anyone who has ever worked in an office knows how easy it is to file something so effectively that it becomes lost for ever! Development of computer networks is helping with this problem, as it is with other problems, but in the past the Soviet planners have disposed of only the most primitive means in trying to solve it.

Then there is the question of the intrinsic content of a given informational category, one which impinges on the very basics of economics. How meaningful is the concept of full capacity, or a norm for materials utilization? Quite apart from the human element, always somewhat unpredictable, there is the dimension of technical progress. Modern industrial economies are by definition systems in which technical dynamism proceeds continuously and at all levels. While the central planners must obviously be fairly well in touch with macro-technological developments, they may only have the vaguest notions about developments at lower levels, especially at the enterprise level, including the implementation of new technologies worked out by the big research institutes. The Soviet system has, then, always operated under a high degree of informational uncertainty, and the importance of this fact cannot be overstressed. It is only against this background that one can come to an understanding of the means whereby the planners approach the problem of plan consistency, and, at a further remove, how the whole system really functions.

The traditional basis on which the central planning organs try to sort out inter-sectoral and inter-product relationships within the plan is the material balances method. An example of a material balance is shown in Table 4:

TABLE 4

Material Balance for Product X for 1968 (000,000s of tons)

Resources	Distribution
1. Production (sub-divided by republics)	1. Production needs (sub-divided by republics and by ministries)
2. Imports	2. Free market allocation
3. Other sources	3. Exports
4. Stocks at suppliers at beginning of plan period (sub-divided by republics)	4. Other needs
	5. Stocks at suppliers at end of year
	6. Reserves

NOTE

Free market allocation refers to supplies which go outside the sphere of state-sector production, i.e. all goods for final consumption, but also producer goods for the collective farm sector.

SOURCE

M. Ellman, 'The consistency of Soviet plans', in M. Bernstein and D. R. Fusfeld, *The Soviet Economy – a book of Readings* (3rd ed.), Irwin, Homewood, Illinois, 1970, p. 87.

What is immediately obvious from the table is that the method is essentially a double-entry book-keeping method, not a matrix method. It is quite impossible to show directly the complex interrelationships of the economy through material balances. It is also quite impossible to use advanced computational techniques in the working out of the balances. It is important to emphasize, however, that the material balances method evolved during the 1930s, at which time no satisfactory matrix-based approach to the problem of consistency had yet been found. Nor, of course, had computers been invented.

At present *Gosplan* works out balances for around 2,000 commodity groups, while *Gossnab* (State Supply Committee), more directly involved with actual allocation of commodities, handles roughly 18,000 different groups.[1] It is clear that, using as clumsy a method as material balances, the working out of interrelationships of around 20,000 commodity groups presents enormous problems. To achieve consistency it is necessary to work through a certain number of iterations when variables in the plan change. If, for example, the production of steel is to be raised, then the production of the inputs into steel must also be raised, as must that of the inputs into the inputs of steel, which will probably include steel itself, and so on. The number of these iterations that must be done in order to obtain a reasonably consistent plan will obviously depend on the structure and complexity of the particular economy in question. When it comes down to putting an actual figure of this magnitude for the Soviet Union, there is, in fact, some disagreement. Levine estimates that between six and thirteen iterations would be necessary.[2] Ellman, on the other hand, considers that only two rounds of iteration would suffice for a reasonable degree of accuracy.[3] It is in any case fairly obvious that the task of trying to achieve even a minimal level of consistency with what amounts to a 20,000 × 20,000 matrix, using such a crude tool as the material balances method, is colossal. Not surprisingly, then, Soviet planners have rarely attempted to pursue iteration beyond a fairly elementary level.

> Because the calculation of changes in the material balances is very labour-intensive, and because in practice there is not enough time for the completion of such work, sometimes only those balances which are linked by first-order relationships are adjusted. As regards

relationships of the second order, and even more so those of the third and fourth order, adjustments in the balances are made only in cases where the magnitudes involved are large.[4] Does this mean that the Soviet planning system simply does not attempt to achieve consistency in plans? In conventional terms the answer is probably yes. But there are certain procedures which Soviet planners use which could be described as alternative ways of achieving consistency.

First of all, let us repeat that the planners face a situation of extreme informational uncertainty. Let us add that the perennial Soviet concern with growth in the aggregate has been reflected in the plan construction as well as the plan implementation stage. Downward adjustment in any form has been viewed with disfavour. It is in this way that the principle of 'taut' planning is transformed into a concrete approach to the consistency problem. The planners have tended to seek adjustment by altering production norms, which may often be extremely dubious in the first place, but always in a direction tending towards overall increases in production. Thus sector A may be required to produce more outputs, or sector B to produce a given level of outputs with less inputs, or both. The issue of tautness does of course raise all sorts of general issues about the very nature of Soviet planning, but discussion of these must be reserved for a later chapter. What we must emphasize at this point is that the techniques used at the plan consistency (or inconsistency!) stage are intimately connected with, and cannot be fully understood outside the context of, the problems presenting themselves at the information-gathering stage. Alteration of norms under conditions of perfect information would be simply meaningless. Under conditions of defective information, alteration can attain a crucial tactical significance. A study of the way in which the planning timetable actually proceeds does, indeed, indicate that the two stages, conceptually quite distinct, are in practice inextricably mixed up. *Gosplan* starts by working out and sending down to the intermediate bodies so-called 'control figures' (*kontrol'nye tsifry*) – very rough indications of the principal proportions of the plan and of expected output levels of key products. On the basis of these the intermediate bodies give their enterprises a rough idea of what the demands of the plan are likely to be, and what resources will be available to help meet them. In turn, enterprises make out

indents (*zayavki*) for supplies which they think they will need.
These *zayavki*, of course, will almost always contain an element of
'fat'. This is the first stage at which the process starts to deal with
specific products. The ministries, etc. then aggregate this data
and present it back to the central planners. Next *Gosplan* and
Gossnab attempt, through what often seems to come fairly close
to a process of negotiation, to reconcile conflicting demands,
guess what true capabilities are, and arrive at some kind of
integrated plan, all more or less simultaneously.

Soviet plans are always late. Enterprises commonly have to go
the first quarter of the year without a confirmed plan having been
sent back down the hierarchy. Even so, plans are frequently
changed in the course of the plan period. In Orenburg *oblast*[1]
during the first nine months of 1969, for example, almost half the
total number of enterprises had their sales plans changed, about
20 per cent had them changed three times, and some even up to
six times.[5] Over an identical period, at around the same time,
plans for silk-weaving in Uzbekistan were changed eight times,
and those for silk-winding in the same republic five times.[6]
While this is always deplored by enterprise managements, and by
Western and Soviet economists, it is important to note that what
we really have here is the extension of the adjustment process
into the operational period – indeed something approaching,
perhaps, a crude form of continual adjustment process.

It is perfectly clear that a policy of trying to cope with plan
inconsistencies by merely telling some people to produce more
and some to utilize less is in danger of producing complete
dislocation. That this has not occurred, at least on a large scale,
is to a great extent due to the operation of the priority principle.
In the event of the fulfilment of the planners' demands in the
priority sectors – i.e. historically the heavy industrial sectors –
becoming manifestly improbable, resources have simply been
switched out of some non-priority sector into the ailing or over-
taxed priority sector. The post-Stalin period has, in fact, brought
with it a multiplication of priorities, and the blurring of the
borderline between priority and non-priority sectors, but in
the earlier period the priority principle played a quite crucial
role.

In recent years a new method of achieving consistency in plans
has emerged, namely input–output. Although this technique was

invented by Wassily Leontief, an economist of Russian birth who emigrated to the United States, it did not attract interest among Soviet leaders and planners until the late 1950s. The first input–output table describing the Soviet economy was published in 1961. It covered the 1959 economy, using eighty-three industrial groupings, and has been followed by many more tables, both national and regional.[7]

The essence of input–output is simple enough. By setting out production coefficient material in the form of a matrix, it is possible to find a fully consistent solution through the mathematical technique known as inversion. The important thing is that by attacking the problem in this way it is possible to enlist the aid of electronic computers, a recourse not available with the material balances method.

Input–output has, however, so far failed to replace material balances in the sphere of operational planning. There are a number of reasons for this. Firstly, there is clearly a strong argument that in the context of severe informational uncertainty the advantage of a more sophisticated computational technique is dubious. Secondly, there is the constraint of the limitations of the present level of Soviet computer technique. It is simply not possible with Soviet hardware to invert matrices of 20,000 × 20,000, though this constraint may, of course, be removed in the fairly near future.

Thirdly, there is the problem of statistical definitions. Input–output demands figures worked out for product groups, i.e. technologically determined definitions. Soviet statistics have in general been collected on the basis of industries, i.e. using essentially administrative definitions. As we shall see later, there has always been a strong tendency for ministries, enterprises, etc. to accumulate ancillary activities. Because of this the difference beween product and industry definitions may be of considerable quantitative importance. Obviously industry statistics can be adjusted to bring them into line with product statistics, but when it comes to the stage of setting actual plans they must all be translated back again, since plans are set for ministries, etc. and enterprises. Similar, though less essential, difficulties have arisen in connection with sets of prices used and specific forms of indicators.[8]

Lastly, and in some ways most fundamentally, there is the basic limitation of input–output as a technique. It operates in terms of fixed technological coefficients, i.e. it ignores any possibilities of economies of scale, substitution, etc. So, of course, does the material balances method. But in practice material balances works in such a flexible (one might say almost subjective) way that crude allowances for this sort of thing can be made. Input–output can cope with the problem only through the formal introduction of linear programming elements. What emerges from these specific points is that the possibility of applying input–output is very much dependent on more general issues affecting the Soviet system. Informational problems are largely a function of the high degree of centralization and the command basis of plan implementation. The limitation of matrix sizes could obviously be solved by decentralization. The dangers of the fixed-coefficient assumption can be avoided by transition to an integrated 'optimal' approach to planning. As we shall see shortly, however, this point is in practice not independent of the decentralization issue. Statistical problems, while to some extent purely technical, are also partly tied up with the essential characteristics of the plan implementation system. The discussion of the application of input–output should, then, be seen as an integral part of the whole controversy over decentralization and means of plan implementation, to which we shall return for detailed discussion later.

Now we come to the question of resource allocation – not in any sense logically posterior to the matters already discussed, but much more difficult and controversial in nature. There are two principal difficulties. Firstly, it is often not easy to discover by what means allocation decisions are made. Secondly, and more fundamentally, there is the problem of means and ends. It is perhaps worth pausing to discuss the essence of this problem in detail.

There is a perfectly clear distinction in economic theory between the determinants of the welfare function and the rules for achieving an efficient allocation of resources. The former tell us what is desirable, while the latter tell us how the desirable is to be achieved. In practice the borderlines between the two can be expected to be somewhat fuzzy. In the case of Soviet planning procedures, however, the whole issue is completely confused because the principal plan targets are given out as targets for intermediate goods, not for final goods. Now it is easy enough to understand this, and even, with reservations, to approve it, in the context of considerations of growth strategy, i.e. in macro-economic terms. But it does mean that there is no unique bundle of final goods to which planners can refer in attempting to gauge the extent to which the desirable has been achieved.

We can, perhaps, presume that, whatever the position during the 'heroic' days, contemporary Soviet planners/politicians have some idea, when expounding targets for steel, coal, etc., of the final uses to which these will be put. We can certainly reasonably think in terms of the existence of an implicit rate of time preference – without, of course, suggesting that the rate necessarily reflects the preferences of the Soviet population. But when it comes to strategic decisions about the relative weight of different sectors – say, coal/oil/gas – there is really very little we can say in the way of generalization, except that what are usually referred to as 'political' factors may well be of crucial importance. If we drop the level of generality a little to that of specific investment projects, it is possible to pinpoint principles which influence resource allocation decisions, but they are principles, rather than techniques, so it is best to set them aside for discussion in Chapters Five and Eight where the whole problem of investment strategy will be tackled.

At the other end of the scale – the level of factory-floor production decisions – we are again in difficulties, though for quite different reasons. A certain and, since 1965, increasing degree of freedom is formally allowed to factory management to make autonomous decisions on processes and even, to a limited extent, on assortment of final production. In addition, there have always been significant elements of informal, or even downright illegal, decentralized decision-making, as we shall see later. Again, intermediate bodies often seriously affect resource allocation patterns in ways basically explicable in terms of organizational, rather than national-economic considerations. But to the extent that decisions on these matters are effectively taken by central planning bodies, and assuming that the requisite information is to hand, which it is unlikely to be, we are faced with the question of whether those bodies can have time to take them on any consistent, organized basis. The planners do, after all, have enough on their plates with other matters, and our previous discussion of the problems of trying to achieve plan consistency surely indicates that production profiles, etc. are switched around basically in order to get more short-term output of a particular product, rather than to improve the allocation of resources as such.

With the intermediate kind of allocation decision – decisions on which technique to use in the implementation of a given investment project, e.g. hydro versus thermal power generation – we are on rather more solid ground. Intermediate bodies do, certainly, have a significant degree of control over this type of decision-taking as well, but there are formal rules on the basis of which design organizations (*proektnye organizatsii*) are supposed to work out plans for new projects. Once again, of course, design organizations have their own axes to grind, so that we cannot talk of 'pure' decision-making at this level either. But the formal rules do matter (even though they have never been made legally obligatory) and have mattered increasingly over the course of Soviet economic history.

The origins of the 'Coefficient of Relative Effectiveness' (CRE), a kind of modified pay-off period technique, go back to the 1930s. Even in those days of 'voluntarism' it was felt necessary to have some basis for deciding between alternative projects in sectors like power generation and transport construction – sectors in general very highly capital-intensive, but with considerable variations in the degree of that capital intensity, depending on the precise technique used.[9] It was not, however, until 1958 that an all-union conference on 'problems of determining the economic effectiveness of capital investment and new technology' was held, following which a 'Standard Methodology for Determining the Economic Effectiveness of Capital Investment and New Technology in the National Economy of the USSR' was published.[10] A revised version of this standard methodology appeared in 1969,[11] without changing any of the fundamental characteristics of the CRE method.

The method is based on the expression:

1. e greater or less than E, where e equals $\dfrac{C_2 \text{ minus } C_1}{K_1 \text{ minus } K_2}$,

and K is capital expenditures, C running costs, including depreciation, and subscripts denote projects to be compared. E is the normative coefficient to which actual coefficients are compared.

Thus E is a quasi-rate of interest and e a quasi-marginal rate of return. An alternative formulation:

2. t greater or less than T, where t equals $\dfrac{K_1 \text{ minus } K_2}{C_2 \text{ minus } C_1}$,

t being the time it takes for a more capital-intensive variant to recompense greater capital costs through economies in running costs, and T the corresponding norm, shows that e is really nothing more than the reciprocal of a marginal recoupment period.

The comparison with conventional Western notions of interest, present value, etc. should not be pushed too far. A pay-off period approach is by definition completely insensitive to varying lifetimes of projects. E is arbitrarily determined, and has usually been below 'clearing' level. In addition, there have been considerable variations between sectors,[12] though a uniform E, at least in principle, is one of the features of the new standard methodology. Finally, it is obvious that in cases where capital costs occur over a number of time periods and/or where running costs are not constant, the method becomes very crude indeed. There are, indeed, more sophisticated versions of the CRE which take account of these limitations,[13] but it is not clear to what extent these are in fact used. What can be said about all Soviet comparative effectiveness approaches is that they tend to favour excessive capital intensity, thus perhaps strengthening tendencies which exist in any case, for ideological reasons. But one should not proceed from the fact that the formal concept of rate of interest and indeed the institution of an actual capital charge came as late as 1965, to the assumption that forms of shadow rate of interest have been wholly lacking throughout most of Soviet economic history.

Soviet theoretical economics had a hard time during the Stalin period, and as late as 1952 Stalin himself wrote: 'Problems of rational organization of productive forces, planning of the national economy etc., are not the subject of political economy, but of the economic policy of the directing organs.'[14] In other words, anything to do with actual decision-taking, applied or theoretical, was no business of economists. Since the death of Iosef Vissarionovich, however, political relaxation and increasing concern with considerations of micro-economic efficiency have combined to produce a rebirth of economics as a policy science in the

Soviet Union. In point of fact, economics never really died. Theoreticians like Nemchinov continued to work quietly through the 1920s, 1930s and 1940s, and Lev Kantorovich in fact invented linear programming as early as 1938, eight years before its independent reinvention in the USA. The invention was not of course taken up, and it was not until the late 1950s that a real and audible movement came into existence, centred on the development of the new mathematical techniques, and led by veterans like Nemchinov and Novozhilov. The movement was concerned with a number of things. It was concerned with input–output, which has already been discussed, and with decentralization, a subject to which we shall be turning shortly. It was also concerned with questions of resource allocation planning.

The intellectual distinction of the debate on 'optimal planning', as it has come to be known, has not however been matched by the extent of its application in actual planning. The story is similar to that of input–output. Many theoretical problems remain to be solved in the field of programming for resource allocation problems. The assumptions of linear programming limit its practical applicability. Dynamic, non-linear programming is still only in the processs of being developed.[15] And once again we find that the issue of planning theory and practice cannot be separated from the general issues of methods of plan implementation and degree of centralization/decentralization. In 1964 two eminent Soviet economists wrote:

> Electronics has brought no really tangible benefit to the planning and management of the economy, principally because planning and management, as organized at the present time, is not adapted to the evolution, and more important the implementation, of optimal decisions.
>
> Let us take an example. It is well known that the compilation of optimal schemes of freight shipment can yield a quite substantial saving. This is not a complicated task. Many articles and books have been written and not a few dissertations defended on the subject. Still, hardly any freight is shipped according to optimal schemes. Why not? Simply because the transport organizations, contrary to the dictates of common sense, are given plans based on ton-kilometres, while optimal schemes minimize ton-kilometres. One can establish computer centres, and conceive superb algorithms, but nothing will come of it as long as transport organizations reckon plan fulfilment in ton-kilometres.[16]

Clearly inescapable difficulties ensue if planners try to graft modern, sophisticated methods of solving allocation problems on to traditional methods of plan implementation. Is it, then, the command principle rather than the degree of centralization as such that constitutes the main barrier to reform? Is there not some way in which programmed price calculations can be used as the basis for a plan implementation process not based on directly technological indicators? In terms of first principles there is, indeed, no real problem. Technical data can be fed into a computer, and optimal output levels discovered, through the use of programming methods. By using duality theorems these data can be used as a basis for calculating the corresponding scarcity prices. The prices can then simply be handed out to enterprise managements, along with an instruction to maximize profits. It is assumed that allowance will be made at the programming stage for external economies, etc.

Unfortunately, there are a number of difficulties with this approach. Firstly, at the purely theoretical level, the assumptions necessary to guarantee a unique level of output corresponding to a given structure of prices are fairly demanding. They include no increasing returns to scale, no externalities, etc. Secondly, there are the practical problems. As was mentioned in Chapter One, the question of what theoretical basis the Soviets use to calculate their prices is really somewhat academic. Even with the most modern computers it is simply not possible to calculate in an organized way thousands upon thousands of prices. The most enlightened Soviet planning authority imaginable would still find that prices had to be set by rule of thumb, and that anomalies are inevitable. It is difficult then to dispute Ellman's conclusion that

> it is easy to write about indirect centralization, about calculating optimal prices which will guide profit maximizing enterprises to socially rational decisions. Such prices do not in general exist, and in practice it is difficult to see how the problems of information and aggregation could be overcome.[17]

In this context it is easy to understand why the most eminent Soviet mathematical economists, front-runners in the development of techniques for programming economic problems, have also tended to be staunch decentralizers. In practical terms the evolution of modern methods of resource allocation calculation has provided a basis for rationalization of decision-taking at all levels, but has not significantly affected the basic issues of the relationships between those levels. The general conclusions of this chapter are that (a) Soviet plan construction techniques have been fairly primitive; (b) inherent crudeness in techniques has been intensified directly, owing to the high degree of centralization of the system, and indirectly, through the effect of the command principle; (c) modern mathematical developments, while in principle indicating a possible road to 'perfect computation',[18] have in practice shown greater possibilities in the context of a rationalized, decentralized system. It is with these conclusions in mind that we shall proceed to a detailed examination of Soviet plan implementation procedures.

NOTES

1. A. Nove, *The Soviet Economy*, 3rd edition, p. 92.
2. H. S. Levine, 'The centralized planning of supply in Soviet industry', in eds. M. Bornstein and D. R. Fusfeld, *The Soviet Economy – a Book of Readings*, 2nd ed., Irwin, Homewood, Illinois, 1966, p. 55.
3. M. Ellman, 'The consistency of Soviet plans', in Bornstein and Fusfeld, *The Soviet Economy* ..., p. 87.
4. A N. Yefimov, *Perestroika Upravleniya Promyshlennost'yu i Stroitel'stom v SSSR*, Gospolizdat, Moscow, 1957, p. 107, quoted in Levine, *op. cit.*
5. A. Voronov, 'Otvetstvennost' predpriyatiya i glavka', in *Ekonomicheskaya Gazeta*, 1/70, p. 7.
6. Ed. O. B. Dzhamalov, *Ekonomicheskaya Reforma v Promyshlennosti Uzbekistan*, Fan, Tashkent, 1969, p. 128.
7. For a list of the tables that have been constructed see M. Ellman, *Soviet Planning Today*, Cambridge University Press, 1971, pp. 110–111.
8. For further discussion of these points see V. G. Treml, 'A note on Soviet Input–Output tables', in *Soviet Studies*, July 1969.
9. See G. Grossman, 'Scarce capital and Soviet doctrine', in *Quarterly Journal of Economics*, August 1953.
10. *Tipovaya Metodika Opredeleniya Ekonomicheskoi Effektivnosti*

*Kapital'nykh Vlozhenii i Novoi Tekhniki, Gosplan SSSR;
Akademiya Nauk SSSR, Insitut Ekonomiki,* Moscow, 1960.

11. *Tipovaya Metodika Opredeleniya Ekonomicheskoi Effektivnosti
   Kapital'nykh Vlozhenii,* in *Ekonomicheskaya Gazeta,* 39/69.
12. See Vaag, *op. cit.*
13. See A. Bergson, *The Economics of Soviet Planning,* Yale University Press, New Haven and London, 1964, p. 255.
14. I. V. Stalin, *Economic Problems of Socialism,* Foreign Languages Publishing House, Moscow, 1952, p. 72.
15. See W. J. Baumol, *Economic Theory and Operations Analysis,* 2nd ed., Prentice-Hall, Englewood Cliffs, New Jersey, 1965, Chap. 7.
16. V. Belkin and I. Birman, 'Samostoyatel'nost' predpriyatiya i ekonomicheskie stimuly', in *Izvestiya,* 4 December 1964, p. 5.
17. Ellman, *Soviet Planning Today,* pp. 19–20.
18. The term was invented by P. J. D. Wiles. See his *Political Economy of Communism,* Blackwell, Oxford, 1964, Chapter 10.

Plan Implementation in
the 'Classical' Period

We have already stated, as a general principle, that any under-standing of the Soviet system must be based on some kind of dynamic conception. It is particularly important to bear this in mind when discussing methods of plan implementation, and for this reason the subject has been divided up on a more or less linear historical basis. We will come to explicit and detailed discussion of the exact meaning of trends in implementation, dynamically considered, only in the final chapter, but the reader should be prepared to come to his own conclusions as we move through the material.

It is probably fairly reasonable to say that in the beginning, i.e. in the early 1930s, problems of plan construction did not present themselves very forcibly. Heavy emphasis on a few top-priority projects made micro-economics irrelevant, and consistency problems fairly simple of solution. But the problem that did immediately present itself was that of the terms in which to set the plan. In principle, there are two ways in which this problem could have been completely solved. The first is perfect knowledge, detailed targets for every aspect of the production process, and perfect cognizance of the process of implementing these multitudinous instructions. For reasons discussed in Chapter Two this solution was, and remains, out of the question. The second possible total solution would have been in terms of what are called moral incentives (*moral'noe pooshchrenie*). Enterprise managers, etc. would be inspired by socialism, patriotism or other ideals to interpret cryptic commands from the centre in a way conducive to the achievement of some kind of optimum. There are two things wrong with this proposed solution. Firstly, the managers would in most cases not know what was conducive to the optimum. Secondly, the managers might not respond primarily in terms of moral incentives. Quite apart from any consideration of what normally comes under the rubric of human nature, the Soviet authorities have in fact always pursued a policy of combining moral incentives with material incentives, with the latter taking evident priority. It is a fairly safe generalization to say that policy on motivation of managing cadres has been largely based on material incentives throughout the post-1928 period. One estimate is that in the early 1960s total managerial bonuses were averaging 25–33 per cent of basic salary.[1] In 1947 the corresponding figure for the top-priority iron and steel industry was 51·4 per cent.[2]

What about managerial reactions? It has been observed in the West that, while for various reasons profit maximization has ceased to be a very sound hypothesis for predicting managerial behaviour, theories based on some conception of maximization of personal material gain present fairly good bases for prediction.[3] It is appropriate in the case of Soviet executives to propose a specific form of this conception, namely a theory of bonus maximization. Very good predictions are yielded by such a theory. There is little conflict in the Soviet Union between material considerations and status considerations – as we would expect, given that it is the state that organizes the incentive systems and the status symbols. But bear in mind that we could probably say much the same about most Western societies, where that is the case only to a very limited extent. Where the Soviet system is rather different from Western systems is in the absence, to a great extent, of the complication of long-term considerations in the field of prediction of managerial behaviour.

A Western manager who insists on maximizing personal emoluments over a forty-year period may be as much of a headache for the would-be predictor as one who maximizes his number of visits to the golf club. Soviet managers have rarely had time horizons on such a scale. In nine out of the sixteen enterprises surveyed by Richman in the early 1960s, for example, directors had been in their posts for less than four years.[4] In addition, however, the pre-1965 system gave even the stable veteran Soviet manager little incentive to look beyond the current year, quarter, or even month. The basic situation was that (a) a manager had to fulfil his plan in every operational plan period – either one month or one quarter – in order to get regular bonuses and avoid trouble with superiors. The Micawber principle was in operation – 100·1 per cent fulfilment – happiness; 99·9 per cent – misery. While special bonuses were awarded for each percentage point of overfulfilment, these were on a relatively small scale, and underfulfilment meant total loss, rather than proportionate reduction, of the basic fulfilment bonus; (b) the operation of the ratchet principle meant that any attempt to build up a strong long-term position came up against a strong tendency on the part of the planners to react to very good performance figures by jacking up plan targets. Reference back to the discussion of informational problems in Chapter Two will place in perspective this penchant of the planners. Whatever the value of ratchet planning in terms of easing informational problems for the centre might be, however, it was far from conducive to management taking a 'long view'.

What specific patterns of behaviour reflected this basic emphasis on short-run material emoluments as a basis for plan implementation? Here we come to a more detailed discussion of the famous success-indicator problem. Up to 1965 the predominant form of success-indicator was nearly always output, in some form or another. Most commonly, gross output targets were used – gross output being output inclusive of the value or weight, etc., of bought-in materials and semi-finisheds. The whole question of the origin of this predominance, at times reaching the proportions of a 'cult of the gross',[5] is one that we shall be going into later. For the moment it is important only to note that, on paper, gross output was always merely one of many indicators. Enterprises received targets for cost-reduction, assortment, labour productivity, and even profits – in all around thirty planned indicators were sent out. In many cases, however, fulfilment or non-fulfilment of these other indicators had no direct effect on bonus levels. Nor indeed would it have been possible to have a bonus scheme sensitive to over thirty variables. Quite apart from the enormous difficulties that the working-out and administration of such a system would have involved, there is the problem of consistency between the different indicators. Reference back to Chapter Two will remind the reader that a system which struggles so desperately to attain consistency between all the output targets is unlikely to have much time for the far more difficult task of achieving consistency between, say, output targets and productivity targets. It is, then, clear enough why there was a strong tendency for some predominant indicator to emerge.

But other indicators were never meaningless, even in the days before discussion of reform became general. The payment of bonuses was supposedly dependent, for example, on the fulfilment of assortment plans, and it is certainly true that excessively flagrant distortion of assortment, or indeed excessive disregard for costs, quality, etc., sometimes resulted in severe treatment of the management involved, even to the extent of dismissal. But the limited resources and techniques at the disposal of the 'control' sector meant that a shrewd manager could feel his way to a maximum level of distortion which he could fairly safely get away with. We must, then, be careful to speak of tendencies to distorted assortment, etc., bearing in mind that our illustrations are almost always extreme examples which have resulted in the imposition of severe sanctions.

Gross output was measured in various ways. If in physical terms, as was normal with fairly homogeneous products, it might be in tons, area, or number of units. With more heterogeneous products gross output was measured in value terms, i.e. in roubles. Thus we can see clearly the first major form of success-indicator distortion – the distortion of specification. The cartoon in Fig. 1, from the Soviet satirical magazine *Krokodil*, indicates the dangers of plans set in weight. It is of interest that the hideousness of much Soviet architecture in the Stalin period, with its tasteless embellishments, has been blamed partly on the use of a variant of gross output as principal success-indicator in the design sector.[6] The same kind of 'heavy' deviation occurred with reinforced concrete production, though here as a result of use of a volume indicator – in cubic metres.[7]

With gross output set in roubles the obvious danger is an excessive concentration on the more expensive items, and neglect of the cheaper. A standard example is the shortage of children's clothes and shoes that used to prevail, a perverse result of a policy of establishing low prices for such products. It is worth noting that if prices are distorted, not in a resource allocation sense, but

Fig. 1 'I will make everyone bow down before my creation.' (*Krokodil*, 20/1/63, p. 3. Drawings by Yu. Cherapanov)

in the sense of not being set in terms of a standard mark-up percentage, it would be possible with a value gross-output indicator to increase total output without necessarily violating the cost plan, by concentrating on products with higher margins. Only the assortment plan would be violated, and even that not necessarily, since no assortment plan has ever been completely disaggregated.

The second principal problem connected with the gross output success-indicator was that of quality. Obviously a system which lays emphasis on quantitative performance is likely to be unimpressive in qualitative terms. In a sense, this is simply a more generalized conception of the specification problem. But for practical purposes it is perhaps worth keeping separate the issues of whether a good is any good, and whether it is the good you wanted in the first place. There can be no doubt that the success-indicator regime was a major cause of the abysmally low quality of many Soviet consumer goods in the pre-1965 period, but quality problems affected higher-priority sectors as well. The standard of irrigation construction in the North Caucasus in the middle 1960s, for example, was so low as to render whole systems virtually unusable, and the basis of the problem was very clearly the 'gross value of work' indicator being used.[8]

Thirdly, there was the problem of lack of cost consciousness. Costs, unlike quality, are of course fairly easy to specify, and explicit cost plans were always present. No economy could have grown at the rate of the Soviet's if costs had not on the whole been kept down to a fairly reasonable level. But where short-term output and cost considerations clashed, there could be no doubt as to which would come out on top. Some costs could of course be totally ignored, because of the idiosyncracies of the price system. In particular, capital and land were for practical purposes free goods to subordinate bodies. The absence of land rent did, incidentally, mean a considerably bigger externalities problem, bigger even than what we are used to in the West – but more of this later.

These three types of distortion did not, however, operate with equal strength at all times. The planning process is a temporal one, with its own calendar, and the rhythm of planning tended to react with the rhythm of production in a rather perverse way. Specifically, a *sui generis* ultra-short cycle tended to appear. The evocative Russian word for this phenomenon, with a fine combination of Teutonic *scht* and Slavonic *shch*, is *shturmovshchina*. The conventional English translation of 'storming' seems a little anaemic by comparison, so let us stick to the original. Once again the nub of the matter is the Micawber and ratchet effects. Operational production plans were monthly or quarterly, and it was important that the output plan should be fulfilled in each month, rather than there being an alternation between underfulfilment and overfulfilment by a considerable degree. If, accordingly, production was behind schedule with a few days of the plan period to go, it is understandable that an energetic manager would go to almost any lengths to ensure fulfilment. Working round the clock, flying in crucial supplies by special charter[9] – this was the kind of thing that characterized the typical *shturm*. Chartering aircraft does of course cost money, at least 'shadow' money, and a man working a twenty-three-hour day may get a little tired and careless. So cost, quality, and possibly also specification problems would all tend to be intensified while a *shturm* was on. A survey conducted over the period October 1965–March 1966 found that 21–29 per cent of TV sets were produced in the first ten days of the month, 30–33 per cent in the second ten days, and 39–48 per cent in the last ten days. Small wonder that quality tended to deteriorate in the last ten days.[10]

This, then, was the basic success-indicator problem. But the heavy emphasis on short-term output results had other undesirable effects, less immediately obvious, but no less insidious. In particular, there was the problem of induced resistance to innovation. Before going on to discuss this in detail we must emphasize that there is no question of arguing that the Soviet economy has not been a technologically dynamic one. Quite apart from institutions of higher learning, there is a large number of specialized research institutes in the USSR with very high reputations. And the centrally planned system is obviously able directly to enforce technological change in a way that no Western government can, except in special circumstances. There is, then, no reason to be surprised at the immense achievements of the Soviet Union in space research and other fields. The point is, however, that the success-indicator regime has tended to create a periphery → centre force in opposition to the centre → periphery force, and to stifle initiative from the shop floor itself. Sometimes an innovation would simply go against the way in which gross output was measured. In 1965, for example, a textile factory which had successfully developed some synthetic fibres failed to fulfil its gross output plan, set in value terms, because prices for synthetics were set at a lower level than those of conventional materials.[11] Instances of weight-saving innovations running enterprises into trouble because of gross output measured in weight terms were common.

The more general problem, however, existed independently of the specific form of output indicator being used. Once again, its origin lay in the temporal dimension of the planning process. Almost all innovations, great and small, require some break in the production cycle for retooling. The Micawber effect ensured that such a break would be seen in an unfavourable light by management, unless it promised an immediate rise in output rates. The operation of the ratchet principle ensured that there could be no guarantee that long-term gains would recompense for immediate risks.[12]

Once again, however, it must be emphasized that we are not

saying there is never any innovation in the Soviet economy. Indeed, even in the realm of 'small-scale' technology the Soviets have some signal triumphs to their credit. Perhaps the best-known example is in the development of so-called 'group' technology (*gruppovaya tekhnologiya*). This technique, pioneered in the USSR. is very simple in essence. In the forming of jigs, for example, both the quantity of metal and the number of actual cutting operations can be saved by integrating a number of models into some kind of pattern on the metal sheet – fitting the different shapes together in such a way as to get the maximum number of common edges. Recollection of the way in which balsa-wood model aircraft kits are set out gives an excellent impression of the basic idea. Group technology can, of course, be developed to a much more sophisticated level, and the Soviets continue to do this, and to implement developments successfully. Why no problems? Basically because it is possible to retool for group technology overnight, and because the effect on output levels is almost immediate.[13]

Obviously an adequate incentive scheme, in the context of a command system, demands some special reward for innovation. Attempts were, in fact, made to gear the system better to the introduction of new technology, through the setting up of special pricing arrangements and special funds. It is not clear, however, that this kind of measure was ever systematically implemented, and opposite effects were often created because the standard rules for the setting of prices for new products tended to leave prices on the low side.[14] There are other, more fundamental difficulties involved in introducing any kind of specific incentive to innovation, but of that more presently.

We have seen that systematic tendencies towards low quality and bad specification were present in the system of plan implementation. Recollection of Chapter Two will add to this the fact that plans were often left with no greater an approximation to consistency than the hope that great deeds would be done. Now of course in any industrial economy the vast majority of products are produced by industry for industry. Final consumption goods form a relatively small percentage of the total nomenclature in an advanced system. Consequently the direct effects of these perennial problems went far beyond the sphere of immediate consumption. Industrial organizations could not be sure that deliveries from their planned suppliers would be exactly what was required, because of the success-indicator problem, and indeed could not be sure that they would come at all, because of the tautness of plans. This uncertainty was always particularly serious with spare parts, other small components and miscellaneous odds and ends, production of which is obviously not going to be very conducive to output maximization, particularly when output is measured gross. A firm which makes gramophone decks and fittings, but also builds complete gramophones with the aid of bought-in cabinets, amplifiers, etc., will get more gross output for a given amount of effort if it concentrates on complete gramophones. In addition, spare parts often seem just to have been left out of plans altogether, so that they made no contribution to statistical appearances at all. Thus a major feature of the classical Soviet system was a serious degree of generalized supply uncertainty. We must now discuss how subordinate economic organizations tried to cope with this uncertainty.

The most obvious answer is: why not complain? There are, however, a number of difficulties involved in this solution. Firstly, complaints about deliveries which have not even arrived may be of limited value because you cannot have what is not there. With shipments unsuitable for reasons of quality or specification, the case looks more promising, even though there was no possibility of haggling over prices or taking one's custom elsewhere. Why not simply send the lot back? Problem No. 1 is that by so doing one would have run the risk of ending up with no supplies at all. Problem No. 2 is that such an action would not automatically have affected the gross output performance of the supplier. It would, however, in most cases have caused an almighty fuss, and it is after all through the reporting of such fusses that we have learned so much about the Soviet system. The crucial question is, however: how often is an enterprise with its own monthly or quarterly plans to fulfil going to send back a shipment, given that this would almost certainly mean plan underfulfilment in at least one plan period? Once again refer back to the discussion of the Micawber and ratchet effects. It is very important to bear in mind here that, although we do, for obvious reasons, use extreme examples to illustrate the distortive tendencies inherent in the command system, the normal case would be one of only marginal unsuitability or inferiority. Where shipments were totally useless violent response could be on the cards, but even here we have to bear in mind that useless shipments could be very useful in bartering for scarce resources – of this more shortly. For all these reasons, then, organizations were forced to resort to less direct means of coping with their supply difficulties.

The characteristic reaction of the householder dissatisfied with the standards of workmanship of local tradesmen is 'do-it-your-self'. Soviet enterprises reacted to supply uncertainty in much the same way. The phenomenon of the 'dwarf workshop', where bits and pieces would be produced *in situ*, was a universal feature of the system. Virtually every engineering factory had its own castings shop, for instance. Here is an old report on castings production in the comparatively small engineering factories of the isolated Tadzhik republic.

> The present state of castings production in the republic is char-
> acterized by atomization and small-scale production of castings in
> the various factories. The republic has 15 castings shops and sec-
> tions, with an average annual rate of production of about 900 tons
> of good quality castings each. The largest of these are the castings
> shop of the Ordzhonikidze factory, which has capacity for the
> production of 7,000 tons of good-quality castings annually, and
> that of the Traktorodetal[1] factory, which has capacity for the
> production of 8,200 tons annually, though at present this capacity
> is only 39 per cent utilized.[15]

Examples of this sort of thing could be multiplied. A 1964 report noted that 30 per cent of all nuts and bolts were produced in dwarf workshops.[16] But the resources of an enterprise, even a large one, are limited, and it was at the ministerial level that autarkical tendencies were able to develop to their fullest extent. The intermediate bodies, as we shall see later, effectively controlled a considerable proportion of total investment. They were, accordingly, able to build up veritable industrial empires, with their own construction and fitting capacities, and sometimes even tooling establishments. If we go back to 1954, we find *Glavmosstroi* (Main Moscow Construction) being created through the amalga-mation of no less than ninety-four small, presumably largely departmental, construction enterprises.[17] Not surprisingly 'many industrial ministries emphatically oppose(d) this proposal, and want(ed) to retain the small organizations themselves'.[18] We shall see the culmination and degree of success of Khrushchev's cam-paign against departmentalism in the next chapter. Going back much further, to the first five-year plan period, we come across an interesting failure involving an attempt to centralize castings production which makes it clear that 'distortions' in this key branch of industry could go far beyond the 'dwarf' scale of the Tadzhik example.

The Tsentrolit plant of Leningrad was originally designed with a 30,000 ton annual capacity, and was intended primarily to supply the additional iron-casting needs of four Leningrad plants of the turbine and diesel industry. At the end of 1932, three years after construction had begun, none of Tsentrolit's shops were yet working regularly. Moreover, two of the four plants whose needs it had been intended to satisfy had been shifted to the jurisdiction of a different sub-branch administration (i.e. *glavk* – D.A.D.); these two plants were refusing to contract for iron castings from Tsentrolit and were instead setting out to build their own individual foundry shops. This development left the plans for Tsentrolit up in the air, since its remaining planned customers would absorb no more than 50 per cent of its designed capacity output. At this stage, the Tsentrolit management was planning for production of 60,000 tons of castings by 1936, intending to supply miscellaneous Leningrad firms; but Tsentrolit's superior administrative organ had a substantially lower capacity target, predicted on the basis that the plant would supply only firms of its own sub-branch.

Sometime between 1933 and 1937, Tsentrolit was transferred into the jurisdiction of the machine-tool and tooling sub-branch. It shipped thousands of tons of castings to plants of this sub-branch located outside of Leningrad. It was still finding trouble in gaining acceptance from Leningrad machine-tool plants, and in late 1936 these forced the drastic reduction of its designed capacity to only 9,000 tons annually. (What was involved here was clearly inter-factory competition for investment funds earmarked for foundry facilities.) In April 1937, the Commissar of Heavy Industry temporarily threw out the entire concept of a plant producing only castings: he ordered that a factory producing heavy machine tools should be built immediately on the site of Tsentrolit, using the foundry facilities simply to supply its own needs. It is not known whether this order was ever carried out, but it is relevant that in 1940 Tsentrolit was under the jurisdiction of the heavy machine-tool branch.[19]

Chopping and changing of production profile, as lines of subordination changed, was indeed a basic characteristic of the first ministerial period. The Ordzhonikidze engineering factory of Tadzhikistan was originally established in 1933 as a small-scale repair station, presumably to service the machinery, particularly the agricultural machinery, of this cotton-growing republic. In 1942, however, it was taken over by the ministry for the oil industry – note, a non-engineering ministry – and switched over to the production of heavy-gauge oil fittings (*neftyanaya armatura*). Now production of oil in Tadzhikistan was, and remains to this day, insignificant. But the oil ministry was clearly concerned to safeguard its supply of engineering products necessary in oil extraction, and was prepared to go all the way to Tadzhikistan to do so.[20] This particular example brings out the point that autarkical tendencies have had serious effects on the whole pattern of location of economic activity in the Soviet Union, an aspect we will be looking at in greater detail in Chapter Five.

Autarkical practices undoubtedly aided subordinate organizations greatly in their efforts to stabilize the supply situation. But they did so only at a considerable cost. Economies of scale were obviously sacrificed, while transport patterns often became grossly distorted, with a high incidence of cross-hauls. We shall return to the question of the costs of making the system workable at the end of the chapter.

There were other ways of trying to cope with the supply problem. As the system developed it became clear that the professional Party *apparatchiki*, particularly *raion*, *oblast*[1] and city committee secretaries, would play a crucial role in 'oiling the wheels'. Now this is a most difficult phenomenon to analyse, because the position of the *apparatchik* was fundamentally ambivalent. As already mentioned, the local Party man is supposed to fulfil the function of watchdog, of outpost of the central command, at the periphery. He is supposed to be on the look out for, and to stamp out, any 'non-state' tendencies manifesting themselves in his parish. On the other hand, his reputation and career prospects have always tended to rise and fall with the economic performance of his area, and in the Stalin period that economic performance was measured in gross output. In addition, of course, he would be aware that, whatever the specific instructions and constraints imposed by the central authorities, their predominant concern was with economic growth, and that he would best fulfil his duty to the party by doing everything possible to foster economic growth in his organization and area. It is not surprising then that a local Party secretary might, in addition to occasionally winking at distortions of assortment and reporting, take a very active interest in the question of keeping the local economy turning over, in the face of supply uncertainty. The following quotation gives some of the flavour of the situation.

> In the reception room of the deputy director for supply of the Kuznetsk Metallurgy Combine we happened to meet Comrade Ivanov, an instructor in the heavy industry department of the Kemerovo *obkom*.
>
> 'As usual, I'm pushing things through,' explained Comrade Ivanov, as if justifying his presence here ... In his briefcase lay a sheaf of letters and telegrams addressed to the party *obkom* from different departments. They were requests to 'push through' or to 'speed up' an order for beams, for sheet steel, for steel structures, etc. ... In the heavy industry department of the Kemerovo party *obkom* things are so organized that workers in the department frequently end up as intercessors – pushing through various kinds of *naryad* and other economic matters. When visiting enterprises, they call frequently on director or head engineer, but scarcely throw a glance in the direction of the primary party organizations.[21]

But however much the party man might be prepared to bend rules, and respect the spirit rather than the letter of instructions, he would hardly have gone against the basic priorities established by the central authorities. It is hard to imagine a party secretary of the 1930s and 1940s 'pushing' vigorously for light industry, unless there were special circumstances. But just as, no doubt, not all party secretaries were pushers, so not all pushers were party secretaries. The *tolkach* (literally simply 'pusher') was a generalized feature of the system, and his name was legion.

It was not uncommon for enterprises to have individuals on their books whose sole function seemed to be to go round the country, 'waiting in ministerial reception rooms', etc., and arrange deals of varying degrees of respectability in the supply field. It is not clear how often outright bribery and malfeasance would be involved. It is important to bear in mind that, because of the specification aspect of the success-indicator problem and also of basic problems of plan construction, deliveries would occasionally be of perfectly adequate quality, but lack any direct connection with the production tasks facing the given enterprise. Thus enterprises might end up with stocks of goods, including capital goods, which they could not use, but which were not in general unusable. Given that in most cases there was no question of paying interest at any significant level on such stocks,[22] it is not surprising that enterprises were often prepared to hang on to them. The possibility of arranging mutually advantageous 'swaps' with other enterprises provided the rationale for a 'positive' hoarding policy. A 1963 report, for example, documents the swapping of different types of metal, of ammonia for coal, and of metal for spare parts.[23]

This, then, is the background that provides the key to an understanding of hoarding. But barter was not the only string to the bow of the *tolkach*. Sometimes a much more subtle mechanism, involving the exchange of favours, real, putative or discounted, provided the crucial vehicle. As Berliner has said, 'The term *blat* ... is one of those many flavoured words which are so intimate a part of a particular culture that they can be only awkwardly rendered in the language of another.'[24] We shall not try, but merely emphasize the tremendous importance of *blat* in the Soviet system.

The *tolkach* function was not limited to these 'professionals'. Production management itself often became intimately involved in pushing operations – obviously a high-ranking production man might have better *blat* than someone more definitely of the 'spivvy' type. The position of chief engineer seems often to have been essentially that of 'super-*tolkach*', while covering up for pushing activities, as well as other forms of rule-bending, was a major role of the chief accountant.[25] It is, then, difficult to exaggerate the importance of the *tolkach* function.

How can we sum up the nature of these various ways in which enterprises and ministries tried to cope with the problems presented to them? In one sentence we can say that subordinate bodies did in semi-official and semi-legal ways try to alleviate one group of perennial problems, namely that of co-ordinating production programmes with demand for goods and services, but in so doing exacerbated the other major problem area – the tendency to deviate from least-cost solutions. As already pointed out, dwarf workshops and departmentalism led to loss of economies of scale and excessive transport costs. The *tolkach* obviously does not live on air, and a chief engineer who spends most of his time pushing does not spend most of his time looking after capital stock and keeping his professional knowledge up to scratch. Only the party *apparatchik* can be described as a costless pusher, since we can take his prior existence as politically given. This points to a very important conclusion. While the supply problem and the cost problem can be analytically separated, they interact in practice, so that it is extremely difficult to distinguish between the effects of the one and the other on performance. We shall have to bear this in mind in the course of the discussion of the background to the economic reforms of the late 1950s and 1960s, which forms the first part of the next chapter, and again when we are trying to come to some conclusions on the fundamental nature of problems of the command economy.

NOTES

1. B. Richman, *Soviet Management*, Prentice-Hall, Englewood Cliffs, 1965, pp. 134–135.
2. J. S. Berliner, 'Managerial incentives and decision-making: a comparison of the United States and the Soviet Union', in Bornstein and Fusfeld, *The Soviet Economy* ..., 2nd ed., p. 116.
3. See W. J. Baumol, *op. cit.*, Chap. 13.
4. Richman, *op. cit.*, p. 136.
5. The term *kul't vala* seems to originate from D. Kondrashev. See his *Tsenoobrazovanie v Promyshlennosti, Gosfinizdat*, Moscow, 1956, p. 32.
6. Ed. P. D. Podshivalenko, *Ekonomika Stroitel'stva, Izdatel'stvo politcheskoi literatury*, Moscow, 1965, p. 140.
7. K. Nikulin, 'Voprosy razvitiya promyshlennosti stroitel'nykh materialov', in *Planovoe Khozyaistvo*, 4/58, p. 48.
8. G. Kalmykov, V. Filipenko, 'Zolotoe dno', in *Don*, 10/66.
9. A notorious case of this, coming in fact from the post-reform period, relates to the Torgmash enterprise of Yoshkar-Ola, which spent 175,000 roubles on such special flights in 1967. See 'S veterkom', in *Pravda*, 2 December 1968, p. 2.
10. See E. Skorodunov, 'O kachestve radiotovarov', in *Sovetskaya Torgovlya*, 9/66, p. 14.
11. V. Demchenko, 'Ne opekat'!', in *Ekonomicheskaya Gazeta*, 13 October 1965, p. 6.
12. For a vivid discussion of this issue see Nove, *The Soviet Economy*, 3rd ed., pp. 181–186.
13. See T. J. Grayson, *An Assessment of Soviet Technological*

PLAN IMPLEMENTATION IN THE 'CLASSICAL' PERIOD

Performance: Three Case Studies, Discussion paper Series RC/B, No. 3, Centre for Russian and East European Studies, University of Birmingham, November 1972.

14. See statement by A. G. Basistov, reported in *Voprosy Ekonomiki*, 7/64, p. 151.

15. R. Rakhimov *et al.*, 'Voprosy spetsializatsii i dal'neishego razvitiya mashinostroitel'noi promyshlennosti Tadzhikistana', in *Voprosy Ekonomiki Narodnogo Khozyaistva Tadzhikistana*, Dushanbe, 1963, pp. 10–11.

16. D. Il'enkov and A. Tsigel'nik, 'Statistika i spetsializatsiya', in *Ekonomicheskaya Gazeta*, 4 April 1964, p. 5.

17. See R. W. Davies, 'The builders' conference', in *Soviet Studies*, April 1955, p. 447.

18. Report of speech by K. M. Sokolov, in *Stroitel'naya Gazeta*, 10 December 1954, p. 3, as quoted in ibid.

19. D. Granick, *Soviet Metal-Fabricating*, University of Wisconsin Press, Madison, Milwaukee and London, pp. 155–156.

20. T. E. Dyrin, V. P. Sherstnev, *Mashinostroitel'naya i Elektrotekhnicheskaya Promyshlennost' Tadzhikistana*, Stalinabad, 1961, pp. 8–9; Rakhimov *et al.*, *op. cit.*, pp. 7–8; ed. I. K. Narzikulov *et al.*, *Ocherki Istorii Narodnogo Khozyaistva Tadzhikistana*, Dushanbe, 1967, pp. 213–214.

21. B. Tarasov, 'Otdel partiinogo komiteta ili khozyaistvennoe vedomstvo', in *Pravda*, 29 July 1950, p. 2.

22. There was no interest charge on fixed capital prior to 1965, except for collective farms. Interest rates on *Gosbank* credits for working capital were extremely low, with a base rate of 2 per cent.

23. T. Leshukov, 'Net, vopros ostalsya otkrytym ...', in *Ekonomicheskaya Gazeta*, 23 February 1963, p. 37.

24. J. S. Berliner, *Factory and Manager in the USSR*, Harvard University Press, Cambridge, Mass., 1957, p. 182.

25. *Ibidem*, pp. 215–216; on the engineer as *tolkach* see 'Pochemu inzhener ukhodit iz tsekha', in *Literaturnaya Gazeta*, 31 July 1965, pp. 1–2.

[53]

CHAPTER FOUR

The Reforms and After

After a few years of 'collective leadership', following on the death of Stalin in 1953, N. S. Khrushchev began to emerge as *primus inter pares*. As we shall see later, Khrushchev's first interests had been in agriculture, but he soon began to extend these to planning problems in the non-farm sector. Growth rates during the period 1950–58 continued at the high levels set in previous years, but certain disquieting tendencies were beginning to show themselves. The marginal productivity of capital appears to have fallen continuously throughout these years,[1] suggesting intensifying problems of efficiency in new investment. The thing which Khrushchev fastened on as demanding action was the wastefulness induced by the self-sufficient empires which the industrial ministries had been building up in their quest for security of supply. His animus against the ministerial constellation was not exclusively a matter of economic policy. The so-called 'anti-Party group', led by Malenkov, Kaganovich and Molotov, which challenged Khrushchev's emerging supremacy in 1956–57, was to a great extent based in the ministerial hierarchy.[2] But there is no question of the *sovnarkhoz* reform of 1957 being anything but a serious piece of economic policy.

All the industrial ministries, with the exception of those for power and 'medium machine-building' (probably nuclear weapons), were abolished. In their place were established 103 regional economic councils (the Russian word *sovnarkhoz* is short for *sovet narodnogo khozyaistva* – council of national economy), each controlling the bulk of industrial and construction activity within its area. Sure enough, transport patterns started to change in the direction of greater economy, and the worst excesses of departmentalism were excised. Very soon, however, new, or apparently new, problems started to appear. These problems were subsumed under the general title of localism (*mestnichestvo*). *Sovnarkhozy* were showing a strong tendency to concentrate attention on their own production affairs, to the exclusion of any consideration of those of other *sovnarkhozy*. What was happening, of course, was that problems of supply uncertainty were inducing the new regional bodies to go for self-sufficiency in just the same way as had the ministries. The switch from vertical to horizontal naturally meant a change in the form of autarky, but none in its fundamental nature.[3]

Attempts to curb these localistic tendencies quickly took the form of modifications to the new system. In 1958 punitive measures were introduced against failure to meet major delivery obligations to other *sovnarkhozy*. So-called 'state committees of the Council of Ministers' grew in numbers, and to some extent operated as renascent ministries.[4] Supply planning was increasingly concentrated in new bodies like republican *sovnarkhozy*, created in 1960, and *sovnarkhoz* USSR, which appeared in early 1963. Indeed by 1962 the *sovnarkhoz* of the Estonian republic controlled the allocation of only 0·2 per cent of production on its territory.[5] It is clear that under the proliferation of new planning bodies in the early 1960s was hidden the effective demise of the *sovnarkhoz* system. It is misleading to refer to this process as a recentralization, just as it is misleading to refer to the original reform as a decentralization. The concept of decentralization is meaningful in economics with reference to the position of the actual producing unit, and that position was not changed one whit by the *sovnarkhoz* reform. What happened, then, is simply that functions which had been devolved to the regions were reconcentrated in Moscow. To say that no economic decentralization and recentralization were involved is not, of course, to say that a certain political decentralization and recentralization may not have paralleled the economic changes.[6]

We shall leave the question of why the *sovnarkhoz* system appears to have had more pernicious side-effects than the ministerial to the next chapter, when we shall discuss investment and location specifically. The important point to note in the present context is that Khrushchev's first attempt at reform really missed the point. Rather than going for the root cause of economic difficulties, the First Secretary had attacked tendencies which simply represented the attempts of subordinate bodies to cope with the realities of the system. It was inevitable that such a superficial approach should backfire.

Soviet economists writing apropos of the *sovnarkhoz* reform in 1957 had warned of the need to turn attention to the position of the enterprise, as the crucial variable in any meaningful economic reform. In 1959 a measure was taken which, though of no great importance in itself, represented the first attempt to come to grips with the success-indicator problem. In an effort to attack the lack of proper cost constraints implicit in the dominance of the gross-output success-indicator, cost reduction was introduced as a major success-indicator. The precise arrangement introduced was as follows: gross output targets would still have to be ful-filled, as a precondition for receiving the basic bonus. Incremental bonuses, however, would be received for overfulfilment of the cost reduction target, and not, in the majority of cases, for overfulfilment of the gross output target.[7]

But the new indicator turned out to be less than a panacea. A 1965 report notes, for example, the case of the Podolsk sewing machine factory, where by 1964 stocks of unsold machines had reached 2 million – equal to its level of production per annum. The deterioration of quality which was one of the principal reasons for this state of affairs was blamed on the planners' continual insistence on greater and greater cost reductions.[8]

The nature of the difficulty is obvious enough. Introduce a cost reduction success-indicator and you will certainly stop any tendencies to ignore cost constraints. But you will introduce no greater incentive to study customers' needs, and indeed you may introduce a positive disincentive. Low-cost models and grades will obviously be favoured, while material inputs may be skimped on, thus resulting in a general lowering of quality. One set of perennial gross output problems may be alleviated, but only at the cost of intensifying the other set.

Other success-indicators were introduced on an experimental basis in the late 1950s – a form of value-added indicator was, for example, tried out in some light-industrial enterprises,[9] but no satisfactory alternative was found to the old gross output system. The Khrushchev reforms, then, were in themselves a failure. But it should be noted that a kind of learning process was going on. The *sovnarkhoz* reform showed that mere administrative reshuffling would achieve nothing, and helped to throw light on the crucial importance of the position of the producing unit. The abortive success-indicator reforms indicated that there would be no salvation in substituting one simple, i.e. essentially technological, indicator for another, or trying to combine a limited number of such indicators. It became clear that it would be necessary to try to evolve some kind of synthetic indicator, an indicator which would gain in comprehensive reflection of the implications of the production/exchange process what it would inevitably lose in terms of direct relationship to that process.

This, then, is the background to the emergence, in the early 1960s, of the movement among Soviet economists and planners which has come to be known as Libermanism, in honour of Yevsei Liberman, a somewhat obscure professor from a provincial (Khar¹kov) technical college.

The article which Liberman published in *Pravda* in September 1962 was nothing if not vague. The whole issue of the degree of autonomy to be allowed to enterprise managers was essentially side-stepped. The concrete proposal which did catch the eye, not only of Soviet economists and planners, but also of Western journalists, was that profits should in some way be instituted as a principal success-indicator.[10]

The background to the Liberman proposals is the subject of some debate. It has, however, been convincingly argued that Liberman was not so much originator as spokesman for a set of ideas which had been maturing among Soviet economists and planners for some time.[11] The vagueness of the proposals, indeed, may have had more to do with political circumspection than with intellectual fuzziness. Nemchinov, who could be described as the real father of Soviet economic reformism, was prepared to say, in an article published soon after Liberman's first *Pravda* article, that there should be a transition to 'state trading' in producer goods, i.e. that some kind of market system should be established in the intermediate and investment goods sectors.[12] But the reform lobby seems to have felt at that time that, at least in the published writings of the 'front man', the less specificity about the crucial issues of decentralization and modification of the command principle the better.

For all the caution of the economists, however, Khrushchev, in his last years as Soviet leader, approved the mounting of an experiment which was much more radical than anything that had hitherto been tried – the Bolshevichka-Mayak experiment. The system which was tried out in these two textile enterprises – the first in Moscow, the second in Gor'kii – fell in with the Liberman proposals inasmuch as profit was established as major success-indicator, but in the form of the absolute level of profit (*pribyl'*), rather than the rate of profit (*rentabel'nost'*), as Liberman had suggested. What was much more interesting, however, was that these enterprises, and those that followed them as the experiment was extended, were given limited rights of price-fixing, while some flexibility as to contractual relationships between producer and retailer seems to have been permitted.[13]

Just how much could be learnt from this kind of experiment was, of course, limited by the simple fact that 'reformed' enterprises were having to live in an environment which was still dominated by unreformed enterprises. Comprehensive reform did not, however, supervene till after the political demise of Khrushchev.

Just about one year after the change from the *primus inter pares* leadership of Khrushchev to the 'collective leadership' of Brezhnev/Kosygin/Podgorny, the new prime minister gave a speech to a Plenum of the Central Committee of the Communist Party of the Soviet Union in which he outlined plans for a general reform of planning in the industrial sector. The first thing he announced was the formal abolition of the *sovnarkhozy*, and the restoration of the ministerial system, a measure which regularized the situation, and restored a degree of simplicity to the administrative structure. The most important changes, however, affected the enterprise. The total number of planned indicators was cut to seven – sales, rate of profit on capital, level of profit, wages-fund, basic assortment, payments to and from the state budget, and centralized investment. The first three of these were designated as key indicators, i.e. those determining bonuses. The norm would be a combination of sales and rate of profit, with sales being replaced by level of profit for some enterprises. In fact, other permutations have been introduced,[14] but not such as to represent any serious modification of the system.

The supply system was also revamped. A new body called *Gossnab* (State Supply Committee) was created to look after the details of the compilation of the supply plan, leaving *Gosplan* to concentrate on more general matters. Under the jurisdiction of *Gossnab* a network of regional supply depots would be created which would do the actual allocating of specific products. We can see here a concern of the authorities to limit the scope for the ministries and *glavki* to get up to their old departmentalist tricks again.

As mentioned in Chapter One, a new type of grouping of enterprises, the *ob''edinenie* (association) was brought into prominence as part of the Kosygin reform. Another change, affecting the ministerial hierarchy, has in fact operated in a similar way. Sub-divisions of ministries, *glavki*, were progressively to be put on to *khozraschet* ('economic accounting'), i.e. they were to be put on to profit and loss accounts, with formal success-indicator and bonus systems. Clearly the tendency would be for the *ob''edinenie* and *khozraschetnyi glavk* to meet in the middle, as has in fact happened with the giant Ukrbytkhim and Ukrplastika *ob''edineniya*, which now control whole sectors of the chemical industry in the Ukraine.[15] A further decree of 1973 has placed renewed emphasis on the development of the *ob''edinenie*, particularly the 'big' *ob''edinenie*, with the *khozraschetnyi glavk* being restricted in scope to only a few sectors.[16]

The system of investment finance was also changed. Formerly all centralized investment, i.e. investment included in the central plan, had been financed on the basis of non-returnable grants. Two new financing procedures were to be introduced, based respectively on interest-bearing bank loans and retained profits. The old procedure was, however, to be retained for projects with gestation periods of over five years. What this has meant in practice is that a growing proportion of investment involving expansion and development of existing enterprises has been financed on the basis of the new procedures, while the old procedure remains paramount with new projects. The importance of the category of decentralized investment, i.e. investment not subject to any form of direct central or intermediate control, was also to be increased under the reform, and the reader should be careful not to confuse decentralized investment with centralized investment financed from retained profits.

Obviously the implementation of the general reform demanded a price reform. The old price system, with its great, and often arbitrary, variations in margins over costs, and high incidence of planned loss-makers (*planovo-ubytochnye predpriyatiya*), was quite unsuitable for a success-indicator system where profit played a large part. One change that was immediate was the introduction of a capital charge. From now on all enterprises would pay a form of interest on fixed capital, even after actual loans had been liquidated. Comprehensive reform of prices of goods and commodities did, however, have to wait until 1967. The aim of the price reform was in no way to introduce a system of scarcity prices; it was simply to establish some kind of uniformity in profit rates in different sectors and enterprises.[17] Even in this fairly modest aim it did not, however, wholly succeed. Profit rates in light industry still tend to be considerably higher than in heavy industry, and planned loss-makers have not altogether disappeared. Part of the reason why it has been so difficult to liquidate this latter type of anomaly is that the problem of the category of rent remains unresolved. Despite many statements, both unofficial and semi-official, that the introduction of some kind of payment for the use of unique natural advantages is desirable, the only operational innovation has been the introduction of a form of rent payment for extracted materials.[18]

The last major feature of the reform covered the bonus funds themselves. There would now be three incentive funds – the material stimulation fund, the fund for bonuses, individual and collective, as such; the production development fund, for decentralized investment; and the cultural and amenities fund, for housing, etc., very important in view of the perennial shortage of accommodation, especially of good accommodation, in the Soviet Union.[19] The whole basis of incentives was, then, expanded. In addition, the quantitative importance of bonuses, in relation to basic remuneration, was increased. Lastly, shop-floor workers would now receive bonuses from the material-stimulation fund as well as from the wages fund, which had previously been the sole source of shop-floor bonuses.

As we have noted, the enterprises involved in the Bolshevichka-Mayak experiment were granted limited freedom to decide autonomously on price and contractual matters. At the time of the initiation of the reform there was a great deal of talk about 'direct links' (*pryamye svyazi*) between producer and customer. In fact, however, no significant degree of such control has been extended to enterprises under the general reform. Wholesale shops have been set up in which spare parts and odds and ends can be more or less freely traded, but the continued shortage of such spare parts, of which more in a moment, has reduced the practical significance of this. In general, direct links have meant that the authorities have encouraged enterprises to work out detailed contracts, indicating precise quality and specification needs, but with prices and suppliers/customers predetermined. On the basis of these long-term contracts, enterprises are being encouraged to sue erring suppliers, through the *Gosarbitrazh* (State Arbitration) system. In addition, fines are now levied for breach of supply obligations.[20] But though this may make some contribution to the solution of quality and specification problems – and there is, as we shall see, evidence that the contribution is fairly small – it does not represent any radical departure from the traditional position.

To put the above into more generalized form: the 1965 reform was a decentralizing reform only to a very limited extent, and involved almost no modification of the command principle. The total number of planned indicators was reduced – but it should always be remembered that 'other' indicators, those apart from the key ones affecting bonuses, had always been of secondary importance, so that the reform removed a nuisance to the manager, rather than fundamentally affecting his scope for decision-making autonomy. The reform certainly did increase the quantitative importance of decentralized investment, which by 1967 accounted for around 20 per cent of all design work in the Uzbek republic.[21] As we shall see later, however, this trend has been seriously qualified by later developments.

Some of these latter details point to a major problem affecting discussion of the 1965 reform as a whole. The reform did not proceed as an integrated, fully thought-out piece of policy. It proceeded in the form of a struggle between reforming and conservative factions among the Soviet elites. It can be perfectly cogently argued that around 1968 the conservatives won, and that it is fundamentally misleading to use the term 'reform' in discussing the post-1968 situation.[22] The present author considers, nevertheless, that however much the spirit of economic policy may have moved back into a more traditional mould over the past few years, a new institutional framework has emerged, and must be analysed as such. As long as we are fully aware that 'reform' is being used as a shorthand for this new framework, rather than as a description of an on-going process, then there is no reason why the term should be dropped. On this basis we can characterize the reform in terms of two basic elements:

(a) An attempt to rationalize the central and intermediate planning structure through a return to the ministerial system, and the creation of the *Gossnab* system.

(b) A thorough reform of the instruments, rather than the method, of plan implementation, involving the introduction of synthetic indicators in a key role, but with the maintenance of output indicators, albeit in a modified form.

How has the Soviet economy performed since 1965? Growth rates have picked up, though not spectacularly, and have averaged a little under 7 per cent since 1965, as compared with around 5 per cent for the period 1961–65.[23] Travellers' reports indicate some improvement in the quality of consumer goods, while recent trends in exports of the more sophisticated types of goods show Soviet industry in a good light.[24] But the evidence is not conclusive that the reform has made a radical difference to the situation. The purely quantitative evidence may be misleading. Good weather, leading to good harvests, has provided a bonus in a number of the post-1965 years. More fundamentally, the late Khrushchev period, with its frantic shuffling and reshuffling, may provide a not altogether suitable point of comparison, though there is no other more suitable. A number of commentators, without disputing that there has been an improvement, have argued that the improvement may be an essentially once-and-for-all one, as capital charges and rate of profit success-indicators force enterprises to 'uncover reserves'. Certainly, if one takes the rate of growth in the period 1968–72, one finds a significant drop in comparison with that in 1965–68. But the most important evidence on the reform is that reports of most of the perennial problems of the Soviet system continue to appear.

On quality and specifications for example, a 1972 report from a Tashkent sports shop indicated an almost total lack of items worth buying. Track suits were badly sewn and patchily dyed, with different lengths of arms and legs. The manager of the shop averred that he would be within his formal rights to send back almost everything he received as sub-standard production.[25] Around the same time it was reported that 2,744 out of 16,379 items supplied by the Blagoveshchensk clothing factory were sent back by the Amur *Rostorgodezhda* (textile wholesale depot). All 240,000 of the ladies' coats delivered by the Vostok enterprise from Khabarovsk met the same fate, as did a consignment of 1,790 dresses from a Tbilisi factory.[26] In Kirgizia in 1971 continual complaints from industrial enterprises were received by the Kirgiz coal wholesale supply organization. In September 1971 the Kentau power station sent seven telegrams refusing to accept deliveries of coal because of its low quality. Production of medium-large coals, for which demand is highest, was actually falling in relative terms.[27] A 1973 report from Kazakhstan again showed in the case of a number of enterprises an almost 100 per cent record for sub-standard production.[28]

Quality and specification, then, may have improved, but they are still a major problem, and it is not surprising in this context that supply difficulties are still common. The spare parts problem continues to be particularly severe, despite the wholesale shops, as the cartoon from *Pravda* (Fig. 2) illustrates.

In such an environment the *tolkach* inevitably survives and indeed flourishes. A letter to *Pravda* from the Ulan-Ude locomotive and wagon repair factory in 1969 complained that

> almost every month we send 'pushers' to Novocherkassk; frequently the top management of the factory and specialized supply workers go off there too. But everything (i.e. supply difficulties – D.A.D.) remains as before.[29]

A general report from 1973 confirms the continued prevalence of 'pushing', but notes that this is inevitable as long as the administrative complexities of supply procurement, and the fundamental uncertainty of supply, persist.[30]

We would expect that the introduction of profit-type success-indicators, coupled with price reform, would curb tendencies to ignore cost considerations, whatever the case on the quality/specification front. Be that as it may, the continued prevalence of

Fig. 2 'The spare parts have come at last!' (*Pravda*, 1/1/69, p. 6)

shturmovshchina indicates that, at least when the pressure is on, the old tendencies reassert themselves. A *Pravda* report in 1969 showed that the famous Bolshevichka itself had been guilty on this count in January of that year, delivering 3 million roubles' worth of men's wear in the first half of the month and 4·5 million in the second. The Salyut factory delivered less than 3·5 million roubles' worth in the first half, and almost 5·2 million in the second. The Moskva factory showed corresponding figures of less than 1 million and almost 2·5 million roubles.[31] Another *Pravda* article at about the same time emphasized supply uncertainty as a reason for the continued prevalence of *shturmovshchina*.[32]

One of the first criticisms to be voiced by Soviet writers after the promulgation of the reform was that the ministries were getting up to their old tricks again.[33] They were interfering in an arbitrary, and now impermissible way in the internal affairs of 'their' enterprises. As late as 1969 there is a report of major items of capital equipment being transferred from one enterprise to another by order of ministerial organs[34] – and this in the context of capital charges and returnable loans for fixed investment! More specifically, ministries were accused of setting their enterprises 'unofficial' gross output targets. This, however, was not altogether surprising, given that the central authorities seem to have been continuing to set the ministries gross output targets! The most important feature of the 'new' ministerial system, however, was the strength with which 'departmentalist' tendencies reasserted themselves – once again, of course, not very surprising, in view of persistent supply problems. Odessa correspondents of *Pravda* noted in 1969 that in the four years preceding – i.e. since the re-establishment of the ministerial system – the number of building and building-maintenance organizations had grown four times, with all of them being under different departments.[35] Enterprises likewise continued to go for self-sufficiency, as was indicated in a study of specialization in Leningrad engineering in 1968. 'Just look what a good guy I am, and how passionately I support the idea of specialization. But for old times' sake – let me build just one wee castings shop at the factory ...'[36] One of the main purposes behind the 1973 decree on the development of the *ob''edinenie* seems undoubtedly to have been the 'rationalization' of departmentalism. Strong *ob''edineniya*, with well-chosen general production profiles, would reduce inter-primary unit deliveries to a minimum, thus making the organization of supplies for both ministries and *Gosplan/Gossnab* much easier, while removing much of the rationale for enterprise dwarf-workshops. Reports do not indicate, however, that the 1973 'mini-reform' has been particularly successful in this respect,[37] and one must wonder whether it can be as long as the underlying problem of supply uncertainty persists.

It has been pointed out by a number of writers that there is a number of specific contradictions in the provisions of the reform – that, for example, situations can arise where there is not enough money in the material stimulation fund to pay out bonuses that have been rightfully earned.[38] Other anomalies exist. The rate of interest on loans for centralized investment is $\frac{1}{2}$ per cent, while the 'capital charge', paid after the liquidation of the loan, is around 6 per cent. Some enterprises continue to receive, quite officially, gross output targets.[39] In addition, it is clear that any attempt to get away from the one-indicator system is bound to run into problems in terms of making different indicators consistent with each other, and consistent with the basic aims of the plan. Finally, as any competent undergraduate will know, though perhaps he is used to seeing the problem in a different form, rate of profit is a bad indicator. The reason it is a bad indicator is the same as the reason why rate of return is a bad technique for ranking projects.[40] An enterprise which has, for any reason, an abnormally high rate of profit, indeed a rate of profit above the notional shadow price of capital (6 per cent?!), may be influenced by such an indicator to reject, or be reluctant to undertake, a project which is 'profitable' in the welfare, or at least in the efficiency sense, even if only marginally so. In the context of (1) uneven 'normal' rates of profit, even after price reform, and (2) increase in the importance of decentralized investment, rate of profit was a peculiarly bad success-indicator to introduce.[41]

Despite all these strictures it is perhaps misleading to place too much emphasis on what could be called the technical side of the reform. Many of the difficulties which have been experienced reflect the very nature of the reform itself.

Let us remind ourselves what the basic characteristics of the reform are: a reformed success-indicator system, a modified ministerial system, and limited elements of decentralization of power to the enterprise, coupled with almost complete maintenance of the command principle. Why has the reformed success-indicator system failed to obviate the old success-indicator problem? Reflection will show that, even in principle, and assuming the absence of technological constraints, the success-indicator problem cannot be obviated simply by changing the nature of the success-indicators themselves. By introducing synthetic indicators, which reflect both the cost (production) and revenue (realization) sides of the economic equation, and by orientating the form of the output target in a direction which makes it more sensitive to customers' needs, the Soviet authorities may be presumed to have gone some way to solving the traditional cost/quality/specification problem. But note:

(1) The sales indicator may be only a marginal improvement over gross output. The difference is that if consignments are actually sent back to the producer, as in the cases from the

THE REFORMS AND AFTER

clothing industry cited earlier, then they no longer count towards plan fulfilment. But under what circumstances can we expect that this would happen? Bearing in mind (a) that most Soviet goods are not rubbish, or totally useless, or sent to the wrong end of the sub-continent – we, like Soviet writers, use extreme cases for didactic purposes! – and (b) that the average Soviet customer is not a final consumer but another industrial enterprise, with its own deadlines to meet and plans to fulfil – once again note the problem of periodicity – can we expect that many consignments will in fact meet this fate? What would happen in a market economy in case of a more or less routine grouse about a consignment? Perhaps insistence on an extra discount, perhaps a threat to take one's custom elsewhere, in an extreme case actually sending the whole lot back – and here we have no externally imposed monthly or quarterly plans to meet! Clearly there is still no real flexibility in a system as long as there is no significant degree of free price formation or freedom of contract. And if we bear in mind that even under the gross output regime mass rejection of consignments usually meant Party/political trouble, whatever its implications for formal plan fulfilment, we may come to the conclusion that the sales indicator, as it has been used, is a very marginal improvement indeed. It has, furthermore, created special problems of its own. An enterprise may find itself quite unjustly penalized because of delay in making payment on the part of the consignee, or even just because *Gosbank* is closed for the weekend![42] The problem of periodicity does, in fact, rear its head in a number of ways. Transport delays can mean that production from period t may not be delivered until well into period t plus 1.[43] More fundamentally, there is a problem with a sales indicator whenever the production process is of fairly long duration. In the extreme case of the building industry it becomes quite useless, and has not in fact been introduced as such, as we shall see in the next chapter.

(2) In the 1965 context profit is not a truly synthetic indicator, but rather a combination indicator – comparison with the definitions of compound and mixture in chemistry may be apposite here. It is a combination of cost indicator, sales indicator and assortment indicator. But these three roles are not properly fused. Just as with the crude cost-reduction indicator, a profit indicator can be improved by skimping on materials, or using shoddy

materials, and customers' power to resist is limited for the reasons already discussed apropos of the sales indicator. Assortment can likewise be distorted, though only to the extent that profit margins vary in a way not consistent with the planners' aims.

It is not surprising, then, that the authorities have, as an integral part of the reform, tried to encourage increased use of litigation as a means of ensuring timely and accurate fulfilment of contracts. The big problem here, however, has been once again the fact that most customers are industrial enterprises rather than final consumers. As a result, fines for infringement of contract tend to be cumulative, and to leave no one much better off or worse off beyond the immediate short run.[44]

Let us repeat that the general problem here is one of principle, not just of practice. We can visualize a system where planners, on the basis of perfect information, produce a totally comprehensive output programme, work out corresponding shadow prices with the aid of duality techniques, and hand down these prices to contractually committed enterprises, with an instruction to maximize profits. Unless one assumes that perfect information includes perfect monitoring, then there will still be the possibility of increasing profits by skimping on materials, etc. Specific features of the Soviet planning system may make the problem more acute, but they do not create it. Just how much flexibility is needed to wholly obviate the success-indicator problem – whether only some degree and/or some combination of free prices and free contracts would be adequate – is essentially a practical issue, and it would be misleading to pretend that an *a priori* answer to it can be given. Perhaps, for example, a limited degree of downward price flexibility is all that would be required. But this brings us on to the general issue of combination of command and market elements in a planning system, and the Soviet planning reform does give us some interesting empirical evidence on necessary conditions for the coexistence of the two principles. In particular, experience since 1965 with the decentralized investment category shows very clearly the kind of difficulties that may arise when planners try to combine predominantly command-based with predominantly market-based regimes within the same sector.

Problems with decentralized investment did, indeed, soon

begin to show themselves. The crux of the matter lies in the fact that, just as no man is an island unto himself, so no part of the economy can be isolated from the other parts. It is all very well to increase the amount of funds at the disposal of enterprises for the purpose of decentralized investment, but where are the supplies going to come from? Supplies are still largely centrally planned and allocated, and by definition you cannot make precise allocations of materials for investment which is undertaken solely on the initiative of the enterprise, and without the need for superior approval. It is not surprising, then, that enterprises have found it extremely difficult to put their decentralized plans into practice. Ostensibly as a way of overcoming this difficulty, a unified plan for centralized and decentralized investment, with corresponding material supply plans, has been worked out for the 1971–75 five-year period,[45] but this sounds more like establishing some measure of central control over decentralized investment rather than really solving the problem, and that interpretation would fit in with indications that the category as such has been falling out of favour, with a consequent drop in its quantitative importance.

It is worth noting in passing that the essence of the problem with the wholesale shops is exactly the same. It is no use establishing a completely free market for bits and pieces if the system used for the sectors producing the bits and pieces is not only not marketized, but remains, as noted above, basically inimical to the production of spare parts.

What, then, would be the conditions for the intra-sectoral coexistence of command and market principles? Clearly, a first condition would be that centralized plans did not press too hard against capacity limitations. Perhaps this excludes the Soviet Union right from the start! Secondly, the sales indicator would have to go. Sales is still a gross indicator, and therefore discourages the production of anything small, and lacking in grossness. Thirdly, and most fundamentally, it is clear that producers would have to be placed in a position where it is not only possible, but actually advantageous for them to produce over-plan batches, in conformity with orders placed by potential decentralized investors, etc. It does, in fact, seem to have been the hope of the Soviet reformers that things would work out in this way. That this hope has been disappointed is largely due to the survival of the ratchet principle in the system. One of the principal aims of the reform was the establishment of long-term profitability norms, which would permit enterprises to get on with production and development, unconstrained by fears that 'too good' performance would jeopardize the position of the enterprise in the longer run. But of course there is still an output target of sorts, and you cannot have long-term norms for output, not even in the form of rates of growth, unless you are prepared to freeze completely the detailed structural characteristics of the economy for years in advance. More fundamentally, despite the build-up of computer networks, the planners are still faced with extreme informational uncertainty, and must still resort to the ratchet as a solid and well-tried, if extremely crude, means of approximation to informational verity. But as long as enterprise managements fear that plan overfulfilment by a wide margin courts the danger of highly exacting tasks in the next plan period, we cannot expect that overplan surpluses will be very common. It would appear, then, that the successful combination of command and market principles on an intra-sectoral basis would demand a degree of overall decentralization sufficient to reduce radically the burden of informational problems on the planners.

We have as yet said nothing about innovation. There were in fact no explicit provisions in the reform covering this problem area. It was clearly expected that the new indicators, particularly those based on profit, would give some incentive to innovate. We can, however, be sceptical about the extent to which this would work in practice, for the same reasons that were put forward earlier in connection with the new indicators and the general success-indicator problem. It is not surprising, then, that a new decree of 1969 returned to the problem of new technology and its introduction. At the 'macro' level research institutes were heavily berated for their lack of close contact with actual production, and instructed to mend their ways. At the enterprise level the approach used was basically that of special bonuses, prices, etc. We have already discussed some of the problems involved in that sort of instrument, and it has been shown that, for example, the highly complex 1969 rules for prices of new machinery may run into all sorts of problems in terms of organizations being stimulated to do the wrong things.[46] We can add that, in addition to purely administrative complexities, there is the problem of simulation. Just as 'new' products are a good way of getting round price control, so they are a good way of earning special innovation bonuses. The more sophisticated the economy, and the greater the emphasis on consumer goods, the greater will be the degree of product differentiation, and so the greater the scope for simulation. It is in any case clear that the grass-roots environment will never be very conducive to innovation as long as short operational plan periods and the ratchet principle survive.

All these things have clearly been in the minds of the Soviet authorities as they worked out the 1973 *ob''edinenie* decree. It is all very well to tell research institutes to get more involved in practical problems, but the new emphasis on administrative integration of research and production, through the medium of the *ob''edinenie*, would seem *a priori* to have more chance of success than mere exhortation. No doubt it is hoped that the *ob''edineniya* will also be 'near' enough to the enterprise to make sure that potential grass-roots resistance to innovation is neutralized, but sufficiently 'far away' to maintain the long view so necessary in matters of research and development. There seems to be some danger, however, that this fine balance may be threatened by excessive 'petty tutelage' over the *ob''edineniya*.[47] Just how well the new arrangements will work out for the R & D sector must await the trial of time.

Some final general points emerge from looking more closely at the operation of the revived ministries. Why were the ministries still, in the early days of the reform, being set gross output targets? Quite simply, presumably, because the central planners still work in gross output terms. Targets for aggregate steel production, aggregate fertilizer production, etc., are, after all, gross output targets. It is output figures, not sales figures, that are fed into an input–output model. An aggregate growth rate is itself a gross-output target. This is not to say that output figures cannot in some way be 'translated' on their way down, but it must be recognized that a fundamental planning problem arises as soon as you try to marry a plan implementation system based on realization to a plan construction system which can only work on the basis of production figures.

Lastly, on the question of renewed tendencies to organizational autarky: it is all very well to criticize the ministries, but the only, or at least the main, reason they do this sort of thing is because the supply system is unreliable. The place for action is in the supply system, not the production hierarchy. If in fact the central authorities did succeed in establishing sufficient control over the ministries so that autarkical tendencies were effectively curbed, the result could be disastrous. This, after all, is one of the ways in which the system copes with a potentially very serious supply problem, and one which must, *ceteris paribus*, become increasingly so, as the economy develops. We can see here that there is a very real danger involved in introducing more effective cost constraints. The more limited the scope of the ministry, enterprise, etc., to go for self-sufficiency, and indeed to send out pushers, indulge in *shturmovshchina*, etc., all of which cost money, or at any rate resources, the more danger there must be, *ceteris paribus*, of supply breakdown.

We are obviously moving into some very difficult general problem areas here, involving the whole nature of the command planning system. We shall leave the discussion at this point, to take it up again in the last chapter. In the meantime, we must look more closely at the sector of the Soviet economy whose activity defines the long-term development of the economy – the investment sector.

NOTES

1. See S. H. Cohn, 'Analysis of the Soviet growth model', in Bornstein and Fusfeld (eds.), *The Soviet Economy – a Book of Reading* (3rd ed.), p. 302.
2. For a discussion of the political aspects of the crisis, see R. Pethybridge, *A Key to Soviet Politics*, Allen & Unwin, London, 1962.
3. For a detailed discussion of the 1957 reform, see O. Hoeffding, 'The Soviet industrial reorganization', in ed. F. D. Holzman, *Readings on the Soviet Economy*, Rand McNally, Chicago, 1962.
4. See A. Nove, *The Soviet Economy* (1st ed.), London, 1961, pp. 74–75; *An Economic History of the USSR*, p. 359.
5. Nove, *The Soviet Economy* (3rd ed.), p. 81.
6. The 1957 reorganization almost certainly enhanced the political power and prestige of local party cadres, and this

may very well have, in some cases, reflected strongly on economic policy. See, for example, Dyker, *op. cit.*, p. 505.

7. For a more detailed discussion, see Richman, *op. cit.*, pp. 139–140.

8. N. Shmelev, 'Chto est' vygoda', in *Ogonek*, 24 October 1965, pp. 4–5.

9. See I. Malyshev, 'O normativnoi stoimosti obrabotki', in *Voprosy Ekonomiki*, 6/65.

10. The slogan, indeed, was so commercial as to result in Liberman being featured, complete with cover portait, in *Time*! See *Time*, 12 February 1965. The original Liberman article was 'Plan, prybyl¹, premii', published in *Pravda*, 9 September 1962, p. 3.

11. See V. G. Treml, 'The politics of "Libermanism"', in *Soviet Studies*, April 1968.

12. V. Nemchinov, 'Planovoe zadanie i material¹noe stimulirovanie', in *Pravda*, 21 September 1962, p. 3.

13. See A. Nove, *The Soviet Economy* (2nd ed.), Allen & Unwin, London, 1965, pp. 251–252.

14. See, for instance, Dzhamalov, *op. cit.*

15. See V. Vukovich, 'Firmy umesto glavkov', in *Izvestiya*, 13 May 1970, p. 3.

16. For a discussion of these latest developments, see A. C. Gorlin, 'The Soviet economic associations', in *Soviet Studies*, January 1974.

17. For a detailed discussion of the price reform, see G. E. Schroeder, 'The 1966–67 Soviet industrial price reform: a study in complications', in *Soviet Studies*, April 1969.

18. See footnote 22 to Chapter One. Note that rental payments established for extractive industries have been proportional to output, rather than in the form of a fixed payment.

19. See T. Sosnovy, 'Housing conditions and urban development in the USSR', in *New Directions in the Soviet Economy*, US Congress Joint Economic Committee, Washington, DC, 1966; D. D. Barry, 'Housing in the USSR: cities and towns', and K-E. Wädekin, 'Housing in the USSR: the countryside', in *Problems of Communism*, May–June 1969; I. G. Tsura, 'Bytovye usloviya vrachei Leningrada', in *Zdravookhranenie Rossiiskoi Federatsii*, 2/71. *Cina*, 29 April 1970, p. 2, abstracted in *ABSEES*, July 1970, p. 116.

20. See M. C. Spechler, 'Decentralizing the Soviet economy: legal regulation of price and quality', in *Soviet Studies*, October 1970.
21. A. Khikmatov, *Rezervy Povysheniya Effektivnosti Kapital'nykh Vlozhenii*, Uzbekistan, Tashkent, 1969, p. 74.
22. This is Ellman's interpretation. See Ellman, *Planning Problems in the USSR*, p. 134.
23. Cf. Table 1. The official Soviet figures for the earlier period are almost certainly seriously inflated. See Nove, 'Some thoughts while reading the Soviet press' and 'Statistical puzzles continue'.
24. For example, the products of the VEF electronics enterprise from Riga. See *Cina*, 3 June 1972, p. 1, abstracted in *ABSEES*, October 1972, p. 41, and, for a discussion of some of the special reasons for the success of the enterprise, I. Dizhbit and V. Petrov, 'Tranzistor: diapazony chutkosti', in *Literaturnaya Gazeta*, 26 July 1972, p. 10.
25. R. Salimova-Prokopenko, *et al.*, 'Bar'eri na puti k pokupke', in *Sovetskii Sport*, 1 April 1972, p. 2.
26. D. Epifanov, 'Bryuki s yumorom', in *Pravda*, 24 April 1972, p. 2.
27. I. Sarkobenov, 'Ugol': kachestvo i assortiment', in *Sovetskaya Kirgiziya*, 5 October 1971, p. 3.
28. Leader in *Kazakhstanskaya Pravda*, 28 March 1973, p. 1.
29. V. Sarzhan, 'Opyat' "avralim"', in *Pravda*, 18 Feburary 1969, p. 2.
30. A. Zakharov, 'Soblyudenie dogovornoi distsipliny – vazhnyi faktor v dele preduprezhdeniya pravonarushenii', in *Sovetskaya Yustitsiya*, 3/73.
31. A. Krivel', 'Shturmovshchina za prilavkom', in *Pravda*, 17 April 1969, p. 3.
32. N. Mironov, 'Anatomiya shturmovshchiny', in *Pravda*, 13 January 1969, p. 2.
33. See P. Rozenko, 'Stupen'yu vysshe', in *Ekonomicheskaya Gazeta*, 5/68, pp. 11–12; P. Noskov, 'Firma i ministerstvo', in *Vechernyaya Moskva*, 30 September 1968, p. 2.
34. Dzhamalov, *op. cit.*, pp. 69–71.
35. F. Koppel', B. Brig, 'Bol'shoi gorod i ministerstva', in *Pravda*, 21 May 1969, p. 2.
36. Yu. Sakharov, N. Petrov, 'Leningradskii eksperiment', Part 3, *Pravda*, 14 May 1969, p. 2.

37. See, for example, E. Golub¹, 'Bol¹shoi konveier', in *Pravda*, 13 May 1974, p. 1.
38. See L. Ovseevich and P. Grodinskii, 'Nekotorye problemy perekhoda na novuya sistemu planirovaniya', in *Planovoe Khozyaistvo*, 6/66.
39. See N. Sklokin, 'Metall: kachestvo, nadezhnost¹', in *Pravda*, 29 January 1969, p. 2; G. Ivanov, 'Kak tonna "pobedila" metr', in *Pravda*, 22 August 1974, p. 2.
40. For a theoretical treatment, see M. M. Dryden, 'Capital budgeting: treatment of uncertainty and investment criteria', in *Scottish Journal of Political Economy*, November 1964.
41. As has been noted by some Soviet economists. See, for example, Ya. Liberman, 'Ekonomicheskaya reforma i finansovoe planirovanie', in *Planovoe Khozyaistvo*, 3/68, pp. 54–55, and P. Bunich, 'Khozyaistvennaya reforma v promyshlennosti: ee osushchestvlenie i nekotorye problemy', in *Voprosy Ekonomiki*, 10/67, p. 47.
42. See F. Yanson, 'O premirovanii rabotnikov predpriyatii', in *Ekonomicheskaya Gazeta*, 1/70, p. 8; A. Kazimov and V. Zheleznyak, 'Nashi predlozheniya', in *Ekonomicheskaya Gazeta*, 18/69, p. 7.
43. See, for example, G. Levakov, 'Eshche o realizatsii', in *Ekonomicheskaya Gazeta*, 4/68, p. 11.
44. See A. D. Vlasyuk, 'Kredit – pomoshchnik i kontroler', in *Trud*, 31 October 1965, p. 3. The effectiveness of legal sanctions has been further reduced by the fact that fines have little direct effect on incentive funds. See Yu. Sedyshev, 'Povyshenie material¹noi otvetstvennosti v promyshlennosti', in *Voprosy Ekonomiki*, 1/70; Yu. Subotskii, 'O povyshenii material¹noi otvetstvennosti pri postavkakh produktsii', in *Planovoe Khozyaistvo*, 1/70.
45. P. Poletaev, 'Kapital¹nye vlozheniya v sel¹skom khozyaistve', in *Voprosy Ekonomiki*, 7/71, p. 54.
46. See M. J. Lavelle, 'The Soviet "New Method" pricing formulae', in *Soviet Studies*, January 1974.
47. See Yu. Zakharov, N. Petrov, 'Ob¹¹edineniya segodnya', in *Pravda*, 7 August 1974, p. 2.

CHAPTER FIVE

Investment

We discussed broad developmental strategy in Chapter One, and have touched on many aspects of the organizational structure of the investment process in the following three chapters. The aim in this chapter is to try to bring together the disparate elements of that process, and to present some kind of comprehensive picture of how specific investment policies tend to emerge in the Soviet Union. But first of all, let us go over the institutional set-up of centralized investment in some detail.

Various central bodies have at various times been entrusted with overall control of centralized investment. The current situation is fairly simple. *Gosplan*, the Council of Ministers itself, and *Gosstroi*, the State Commission for Construction, fulfil this role. A considerable degree of decision-making power in this field is, however, delegated to the ministries, through a rather complicated system of limits. In order to understand this system it is necessary to be clear on the different stages of disaggregation of investment planning.

Until 1969 the planning of most Soviet investment projects was normally based on three stages. Stage one was the so-called 'title list' (*titul'nyi spisok*), which consisted of a summary of the basic characteristics, technical, locational, etc., of the project, usually running to about six pages. Then came the design assignment (*proektnoe zadanie*), which presented a detailed working out of the *titul'nyi spisok*. Finally came the stage of actual working drawings (*rabochie chertezhi*). In the case of very large projects, or projects involving new technology, a fourth stage called the technical design (*tekhnicheskii proekt*) came in between title list and design assignment. But note that in Soviet terminology these variants are referred to, respectively, as two-stage and three-stage design. A decree of 1969 abolished the design assignment, however, and promoted the technical design to the place of paramount importance in the system. It was also specified that in the case of standard projects not involving any special difficulties, the technical design and working drawings stages should be conflated into a single technico-working design.[1]

The general rule has always been that on all big projects the central authorities confirm the title list, while on very big projects they confirm the design assignment/technical design as well – this, for example, was the case with the famous Bratsk hydro-electric station. For smaller projects financed from the central investment funds, the centre merely approves block 'votes' for each sector, i.e. normally each ministry. The exact location of the different limits has varied considerably from period to period. Immediately before 1969 the limit as far as design assignment is concerned was 50 million roubles, possibly with some inter-sectoral variation, and for title list 2·5 million.[2] The current position is identical as far as title list is concerned, but the rule for the new technical design limit is simply couched in terms of 'the largest-scale enterprises and projects'.[3] What this amounts to is that very big projects are examined in detail by the central authorities, other projects above 2·5 million roubles are examined by the central authorities, but not in very much detail. Below that individual projects are simply not examined at all by the central authorities, though overall control of sectoral proportions is retained.

It is clear from a description of these formal regulations that the ministries have a great deal of control over investment matters. In practice they have even more. Quite apart from official limits, it appears to be much easier to get approval for a so-called 'reconstruction and expansion' (*rekonstruktsiya i rasshirenie*), than for a new project as such. The result, which the reader who is becoming familiar with the ways of bureaucratic economy may well guess, is that what are in reality completely new projects are often pushed through the books as reconstructions.[4]

The above picture is complicated by the fact that territorial organs are also involved in approving investment projects. In particular, republican governments frequently have to be consulted by the ministries, and in the case of amenities investment may take the place of the ministry in the decision-making process. With minor projects republican ministries, provincial governments, etc., sometimes take over this role.[5] There can be no doubt, however, that in practice, in any area where power is shared between ministerial and territorial hierarchies, the latter are hard pressed to hold their own.[6] Ministries may be able to exert some influence over the allocation of enterprise decentralized investment funds, but there can be no doubt that this category has given the enterprise a degree of genuine autonomy in the investment field (see discussion of decentralized investment in the last chapter).

The actual work on technical designs and working drawings is carried on by design organizations (*proektnye organizatsii*). The traditional major success-indicator for these organizations was 'volume of design work' – simply a variant of gross output. In 1959 cost reduction was brought in, as it was in industry. Following on the 1965 reform, profit has been introduced as a major success-indicator in one form or another, while experiments have been going on with the introduction of measured work done by completed stages.[7] Even by mid-1974, however, only a small minority of design organizations were 'on the new system'.[8] It is, therefore, fair to say that in general design organizations have worked, and continue to work, on the basis of output unrelated to use-value – sometimes to the extent that targets for the physical number of drawings have been set, giving a direct incentive to the organization concerned to maximize the number of drawings.[9] We can, then, easily conclude that the kind of distortion which normally occurs with gross-output-type indicators will recur here. Sure enough, complaints of low quality in design work and lack of consideration for cost factors, both in the project being designed and in the actual implementation of the design work, have been common. In addition, innovation, whether affecting the technology of the project or the technology of design itself, has tended to be neglected.[10]

The immediate and concrete problem which arises in connection with design work is lateness of delivery of documentation. Obviously the success-indicator system is not well orientated to the study of consumer needs, nor is it conducive to the minimization of the sheer volume of design documentation. But other aspects of the design organization situation contribute to this problem. *Proektrye organizatsii* are perennially overworked, and not only as a function of the general tautness of Soviet planning. Ministries always want to get as many projects as possible started, because it is more difficult to refuse permission to complete, and funds, to on-going projects.[11] Taking the process one stage further back, ministries often commission design work on projects which have not yet been approved.[12] The whole structure of the design organization system tends to be atomized and insensitive to possibilities of economies of scale.[13] Organizational fragmentation, combined with conservatism on techniques of design work, tends seriously to reduce the output potential of the sector below what might be reasonably expected. In addition, hangovers from the days of low levels of sophistication in the average Soviet design worker and the average Soviet construction worker have probably contributed to a situation where tutelage over the design organizations and tutelage of these same organizations over construction organizations has often been excessive. It is difficult to avoid the impression that some of the ninety-one volumes and 70,000 pages of the design for the Novo-Lipetsk metallurgical factory may not have been wholly necessary![14]

Actual implementation of investment plans does, of course, depend on the construction industry. Construction is organized in a similar way to the rest of industry,[15] but there are some peculiarities that are worth noting. As we noted in Chapter One, the basic unit is the trust, rather than the enterprise – many trusts are in fact quite small.[16] In recent years, however, there has been a movement towards organizing building trusts into large-scale *kombinats*.[17] Construction organizations fall into two basic categories – those working on a so-called 'economic basis' (*khozyaistvennyi sposob*), and those working on a contractual basis (*podryadnyi sposob*). The first type is a purely ephemeral organization, set up to do a specific job, and normally going into liquidation on completion of that job. Contractual basis organizations are permanent, some specializing on construction work in a particular sector, some serving a particular area.[18]

As with the design organizations, construction organizations have traditionally used a variant of the gross output success-indicator. 'Gross volume of work' (*valovoi ob¹¹em rabot*) is defined as the total value of work done, including unfinished work, plus the value of bought-in materials. Cost reduction made its appearance as a major success-indicator in the period 1959–65, as in other sectors of the economy. Since 1965 a similar history to that of the design organizations has unfolded. Profit was immediately adopted as major success-indicator, but the work of evolving an alternative way of measuring output was complex. Logic pointed to overall completion as the best approximation to a sales-type indicator, but the nature of the Soviet planning system demanded some kind of breakdown of the process to facilitate monitoring. Accordingly efforts have been concentrated on the concept of 'stages of completed work'. By 1975 more than 2,500 organizations, accounting for about 70 per cent of total contractual basis work, were on the reformed system. It is clear, however, that the concept of stages of completed work is running into many practical difficulties.[19] More generally, there has been a new emphasis on completion of projects, and in 1966 the procedures of the 'State Operationalization Commission' (*Gosudarstvennaya priemochnaya kommissiya*) were tightened up. From now on only actually functioning enterprises would be passed as completed.[20] Complaints about the ineffectuality of the Commission continue, however, to be heard.

Once again, then, we expect, and find, that the orientation of the success-indicator system has tended to result in low quality and/or lack of suitability in construction work. Lack of concern for completion was, and still is, despite counter-measures, perhaps the most important specific form of this. Insensitivity to cost considerations has also been predictably present. It would be wrong, however, to place all the blame for the serious tendency to escalation of estimates exhibited by the Soviet capital investment sector on construction. As we have already seen, design organizations may be equally culpable in this direction, while ministries and enterprises have had little enough incentive in the past to concern themselves with costs. We do in fact find that in construction, as with the design organizations, external factors tend to accentuate tendencies which are primarily attributable to the 'home' success-indicator regime. Supply uncertainty disrupts work schedules, thus contributing to cost and quality problems. The autarkic tendencies of the ministries have made the evolution of a proper pattern of specialization in construction impossible

– obviously the first thing any organization faced with supply uncertainty wants to safeguard is its capacity to reproduce! Atomization in the industry has, in addition to leading to loss of economies in scale, hampered the introduction of new techniques, like critical-path analysis.[21] The quality of labour in Soviet construction has tended to be fairly low, for a mixture of remunerational and sociological reasons.[22] Lastly, construction organizations tend to be faced with an excessive workload for the same reasons as design organizations.

The activities of these various operators in the investment field are subject to various specialized checking organizations. *Gosstroi* has subordinate organizations which monitor the work of both design and construction organizations. The organs of *ekspertiza* which look at design work do not appear, however, to be particularly effective.

> Unfortunately, the organs of *ekspertiza* not only do not inform *Stroibank* about errors and miscalculations in designs, particularly in their economic sections, but frequently recommend for confirmation design assignments in which technico-economic questions are treated in a totally unsatisfactory way.[23]

As we noted, the State Operationalization Commission, which fulfils the corresponding function at the stage of completion of a project, has not been the most powerful of Soviet institutions. *Stroibank*, which handles the finance of all major investment projects except in the collective farm sector, does seem to be able to exercise more meaningful control at both stages, through the rule whereby design documentation, plus a detailed outline of the plan and timetable of work for the year (the so-called *vnutripostroechnyi titul'yi spisok* – 'intra-project title list') must be submitted annually to the bank as a condition of funds being provided. Lateness of delivery of documentation by design organizations must partially emasculate this control, but *Stroibank* seems to have had some degree of success in keeping down escalating costs of projects.[24] On the other hand, the bank seems to have shown little concern with the quality of work, partly no doubt through poor information flows from *ekspertiza*.

Against this background we can proceed to a consideration of Soviet investment patterns in themselves. It is important in studying these patterns to distinguish between those which flow from central policy, and those whose origin lies more in the facts of economic life in the lower reaches of the hierarchy, as discussed in Chapters Three and Four.

One of the outstanding features of the investment scene is the tendency to *raspylenie sredstv* (dispersion of resources). This is a wholly unplanned phenomenon. On average, Soviet investment projects take two to three times longer than planned to complete.[25] Design organizations are partly responsible, through not supplying documentation on time; general supply uncertainty also makes its contribution, while lack of incentive on the part of building organizations to finish represents a further factor. But the ministries have done a great deal of harm in this connection through systematically overbidding for investment funds. In 1966 there were between two and a half and three times as many investment projects under way as the economy could cope with, even given normal rates of completion.[26] Why this overbidding? A number of reasons can be adduced. Firstly, as already noted, the more projects you get going in period 1, the easier it will be to get more investment funds in period 2. Secondly, it is a hedge against supply uncertainty, since the more projects you have on the go the more chance there is of always having something you can in fact complete. But note that overbidding must, in the aggregate, intensify supply uncertainty, thus making things more difficult for construction enterprises! *Raspylenie*, then, creates *raspylenie*. It was hoped that the provisions of the 1965 reform would help to dissipate this tendency, but these hopes have, on the whole, been disappointed. Resurrection of the ministerial system, the continued prevalence of supply uncertainty, the slowness with which reformed principles have been introduced into the design and construction sectors themselves, have ensured the survival of *raspylenie* as a major problem.[27]

Another characteristic of investment patterns that may be readily noted is the penchant for gigantic projects, involving massive investment, often in fairly isolated parts of the Soviet Union. The Urals-Kuznetsk combine and the Bratsk hydro-electric station are good examples of this.[28] All very large projects are, as noted earlier, under the direct supervision of the central authorities, so that this kind of phenomenon cannot be explained by reference to ministerial propensities, etc. In fact, at least three quite separate factors may be at work here. Firstly, the sheer subjective contemplation of a great project may be of considerable psychological importance in any developing country.[29] Secondly, as noted in Chapter Two, Soviet investment appraisal techniques may tend to favour capital intensity unduly. Thirdly, there can be no doubt that the Soviet authorities have often been very concerned with long-term developmental considerations – and in a country of the size and diversity of the Soviet Union the long term may be very long indeed.

Sometimes, however, circumstances have dictated that the authorities take a particularly short view of the investment situation. During the German invasion of the Soviet Union in 1941, for example, the equipment from many factories situated in the path of the invaders was evacuated to the Urals, Siberia and Central Asia. War circumstances demanded that this equipment be put back into production with the least possible delay, and machinery was consequently housed in the first convenient building found, with little consideration of locational factors. These wartime exigencies do, in fact, to a considerable extent explain the rather eccentric pattern of engineering plants in Tashkent, the main city of Central Asia.[30]

But a number of other factors have influenced Soviet location policies, while at the level of small- and medium-sized projects ministries and other intermediate bodies have significantly modified the practical realization of those policies.

Taking central policies first, the official list of 'principles of location of productive forces' gives a fairly good rough idea of the kind of thing that may be important. The list runs as follows:

1. Location of enterprises as near as possible to raw material sources and centres of consumption.
2. Even distribution of economic activity throughout the country.
3. Rational division of labour between economic regions, and complex development of the economy of each region.
4. Raising of the economic and cultural level of all backward national areas to that of the most advanced.
5. Elimination of the distinction between town and country.
6. Strengthening of the defence potential of the country.
7. International division of labour within the socialist bloc.[31]

Apart from long-term economic considerations, already mentioned, these 'principles' introduce a number of other issues, which it may be useful to discuss in more precise and conventional terms.

Let us look first at the strategic factor. Without going into the rights and wrongs of the Cold War and its aftermath, the Sino-Soviet dispute, etc., it is quite clear that the Soviet Union, flanked by the USA and Germany, and with China at her 'underbelly', is compelled to constrain her economic policies by military considerations. Had the Soviet Union been prepared to be dependent on foreign sources for the supply of basic textile materials, the Central Asian region would surely never have become as totally specialized on cotton growing and processing as it is. Were it not for the crucial strategic importance of certain rare non-ferrous metals, the enormously expensive development of Noril'sk, within the Arctic Circle, might never have occurred.[32] More speculatively, the whole development of Siberia may have been heavily influenced by strategic considerations.

Then there is the whole complex of factors which could go under the general rubric of 'internal political'. The totalitarian image of the Soviet Union which still to some extent survives can be peculiarly misleading in the study of regional and locational aspects of Soviet investment patterns. As was discussed earlier, the local Party hierarchy plays a key role in the Soviet system, and a rather ambivalent one. Khrushchev's power was very much among the *apparatchiki*, and the latter rallied bravely to the support of the then First Secretary in his struggle with the 'Anti-Party Group' in 1957. The *sovnarkhoz* reform which followed victory over that group may have represented to some extent a concession or reward to faithful followers. Obviously an *oblast'* secretary whose *oblast'* had just become a *sovnarkhoz* would gain in prestige. It is possible that some of the odder investment projects of the *sovnarkhoz* period, for example the Nurek hydro-electric station in Tadzhikistan,[33] were to some extent the fruit of a situation in which local Party cadres were prepared to use their new position to further what they conceived to be the interests of 'their' area – note that this is quite a different thing from *sovnarkhoz* autarky. More generally, it can be seen that any local Party man with political stature is likely to be able to influence investment patterns in a way more conducive, perhaps, to local rather than national optima, in exactly the same way that local politicians do in other parts of the world.

But local political considerations extend beyond hierarchies to the mass of local populations. The Soviet Union, it must be remembered, is a multi-national state, in which the predominant ethnic group makes up only just over half the total population. And while there can be no doubt that the right of secession which every Union republic has in theory could never in practice be exercised, the authorities have been concerned that local cultures should survive and develop; always, of course, in the spirit of the slogan 'national in form, socialist in content'. This may have induced the authorities to be particularly liberal with investment funds, or at least to go for a greater degree of labour intensity than might otherwise have been expected in non-Russian areas. It is, however, very difficult to get conclusive evidence on the latter point, since the raw material/natural conditions situation (see Map 2) is in any case conducive to a heavy emphasis on agriculture and light industry in the predominantly non-Russian south.

Subjective attitudes to grand projects are, of course, the monopoly neither of capital cities nor of *apparatchiki*, and local pressures based on such attitudes may be broadly enough based. On the whole, however, the authorities have been quite firm on this kind of thing. A good example of firmness is the issue of full-cycle ferrous metallurgy in Central Asia. Central Asia has never had anything more than a smallish metallurgy plant working on scrap iron (at Bekabad). In the light of the total absence of iron ore deposits, and the small extent of coal deposits in Central Asia (see Map 2), this seems a fairly reasonable situation. Central Asian writers, however, have frequently argued strongly, if not cogently, for a change in policy here,[34] but the central authorities have as strongly resisted. On the other hand, the Nurek case is probably one where a combination of broad local sentiment,[35] local political push, and the specific political circumstances of the time, were sufficient in combination to provide an interesting exception.

Now we come to what, from the point of view of the student of planning, is perhaps the most interesting aspect of the investment process in the Soviet planning system, namely the way in which investment patterns are influenced by the needs and modes of action of intermediate bodies. We have already discussed the general issue of autarkical tendencies, and given instances which clearly point to the great importance these tendencies have for investment patterns. It remains to discuss more specifically implications, particularly locational, of these tendencies, and to point out some interesting comparisons between ministerial and *sovnarkhoz* systems in this connection.

Apart from loss of economies of scale, ministerial autarky has always tended to lead to what the Russians call 'long cross-hauls' (*dal'nie perevozki*). The picture of Ministry A supplying its factory X, located in Moscow, from another of its factories Y, located in Vladivostok, about a fortnight away by train, while factory Z, under Ministry B, is making the same supplies only just down the road, is essentially correct, if somewhat overdrawn. The question which obviously arises is: all right, so Ministry A is not going to trust an enterprise under Ministry B, but would it be so difficult to acquire a factory similar to factory Y, but a bit nearer home? In fact there have always been certain factors operating which have tended to induce this dispersed pattern. Firstly, it is more difficult to get permission to build a new plant in a big established industrial centre than somewhere on the periphery. There is at present a list, for the Russian republic alone, of thirty-four towns, plus all the towns in Moscow *oblast*[1], where construction of new or expansion of existing enterprises is forbidden.[36] The ministries have been able to evade this kind of regulation to a considerable extent through 'reconstruction'. But ministries are in general so dependent on 'reconstruction and expansion' as a basis for the pursuance of their sectoral interests that they have had to pick up plants as available, and plants have always tended to be more available in the provinces than in the big centres. They have in any case preferred, for reasons that will be discussed presently, to concentrate their main activities in the big cities, and since a more or less Union-wide network of plants is a centrally imposed constraint for all ministries, the peripheral plants have tended to be left with the little jobs. This has had a very serious effect on locational patterns in the more isolated areas of the Soviet Union. In the Tadzhik republic, for example, engineering factories show an almost complete lack of any complementarity, and are clearly in the main used as suppliers of odds and ends for the bigger plants in the bigger centres. Table 5 indicates the

TABLE 5

Percentage breakdown of deliveries of goods produced at the Traktorodetal[1]
and Avtozapchast[1] factories (Tadzhikistan) to the various economic regions
of the USSR in 1962 (on the basis of gross output)

	Traktorodetal[1]	Avtozapchast[1]
North-west	2·36	0·98
Centre	4·44	3·62
Volga-Vyatka	1·59	1·01
Central Black Earth	2·26	0·57
Volga	2·86	6·35
North Caucasus	11·04	1·74
Transcaucasia	0·11	3·35
Urals	10·22	6·11
Western Siberia	14·69	10·52
Eastern Siberia	9·69	7·00
Far East	8·25	1·39
South, South-west, Don, Dnepr	3·29	0·27
West	0·31	–
Central Asia	11·30	33·11
Kazakhstan	14·20	20·90
Belorussia	0·80	–
Moldavia	0·25	–
Other (export, reserve, etc.)	2·34	3·08

SOURCE
I. V. Chirgadze, *Mashinostroenie Tadzhikistana i Osnovnye Napravleniya ego*
Razvitiya, unpublished dissertation for the degree of Candidate of Eco-
nomic Sciences (Dushanbe, 1965), p. 135.

extent to which two Tadzhik engineering plants used only to a
minor extent to be suppliers to the Central Asian region, let
alone their own republic, but to dispatch deliveries to just about
every other corner of the USSR. A similar situation has prevailed
in the European north.

At the present time almost half of the industrial-production personnel, and about 45 per cent of the industrial-production fixed capital
of the sector, is accounted for by the repair and maintenance
enterprises of the region.

An important task of the future is to free engineering and metal-
working enterprises of the European north from the obligation
to produce things that they could more economically get from
other regions. We have in mind in particular nuts and bolts,
fittings, electrodes, standard spare parts and standard cutting
tools.[37]

[87]

An interesting issue that arises is: why do the effects of autarkical tendencies appear to have been more serious during the *sovnarkhoz* period? Clearly there must be some reason why the system was abandoned so quickly. One possible reason has already emerged. Territorialism left the system more open to sheer economic localism/local nationalism, which can obviously lead to autarkical patterns, quite irrespective of supply problems. Secondly, supply problems were probably intensified during the *sovnarkhoz* period because of the rather clumsy mixture of territorial and sectoral principles which prevailed in supply right from the beginning.[38] Thirdly, *sovnarkhoz* boundaries were very badly drawn, or rather they were not drawn at all, but existing political boundaries simply taken over for a new purpose. The original *sovnarkhozy* corresponded more or less to existing *oblasti*, or small republics, which meant (a) that their boundaries were, from an economic point of view, completely arbitrary, and that the Fergana valley, for example, the main industrial and agricultural centre of Central Asia, was split up between three *sovnarkhozy*; (b) that they were too small anyway to have a very high degree of 'natural' self-sufficiency. It is in principle quite easy to conceive of a system where territorial units, large and with cleverly drawn boundaries, would not violate national optimal conditions to any significant extent by practising autarky in building materials, components, etc., while outstanding major inter-unit deliveries would be sufficiently few in assortment that the central authorities would be able to control them without much difficulty. It may, in fact, be fair to say that the territorial system was never given a fair crack of the whip. Alternatively, it may be argued that Soviet experience indicates just how powerfully political complications may hinder a 'rational' approach to regional planning. Although the number of *sovnarkhozy* was reduced from 103 to 47 in 1962–63, they remained in many cases very small, and the boundaries were as arbitrary as ever. The seventeen 'big' (*krupnyi*) regions that were created, or rather given some economico-administrative reality, in 1961, might have been the basis for something with more potential, but even here arbitrary boundaries caused difficulties. The development of Tyumen¹ oil and gas, for instance, was held up because Tyumen¹ *oblast¹* was originally part of the Urals region. Oil and gas deposits close to the Urals were obviously a much better proposition, as far as that region was concerned, than the richer deposits farther east. In addition, the Urals planners were intent on including Tyumen[1] in their 'own' electricity supply system, which would have meant power going from Europe to Siberia! It was not, in fact, until the *oblast*[1] had been transferred to the West Siberian region that things really started to get moving.[39]

This last piece of empirical material brings us up against another highly important aspect of the whole ministry/*sovnarkhoz* issue. It is clear that the Urals people were concerned not only that the development of the more distant Tyumen[1] deposits would necessarily involve economic links with the immediately contiguous areas to the south and east, rather than with the 'metropolis' area. The other issue involved was the simple fact that the Urals region was already developed, whereas Tyumen[1] was an underdeveloped Siberian wilderness. Why should the Urals go to the bother of building up a completely new urban-industrial complex in a peripheral area, where external benefits would tend to go outside the region?

Before we can go on to a proper study of the problem of externalities in a command system, we must clarify a few points of principle. This will aid the discussion not only of the structure of the investment process, the present topic, but also of general investment strategy, which we will come to in Chapter Eight.[40] Firstly, we should distinguish external economics and diseconomies of scale. This is what Weber called the 'agglomeration factor',[41] and covers essentially locational economies, such as savings on transport expenditures, or diseconomies like the advent of atmospheric pollution as a new urban-industrial area is built up. Secondly, there are external production economies/diseconomies. Under this rubric come diseconomies exemplified by the pollution by factory A, through industrial effluent, of a watercourse which factory B uses as a raw material source. There may be some tendency for economies of this type to be internalized in a market system – e.g. by-products which turn out to be useful to someone are very soon charged for. But we can assume no such tendency in the case of a command system.

There has been considerable controversy among Western economists over the issue of so-called pecuniary externalities.[42] Clearly the construction of a new enterprise in a given area may affect the cost structure of existing enterprises. Opportunities to exploit economies of scale may be presented simply through expansion of the market. Now it is quite correctly argued that such an economy is not, in the context of a market economy, properly included as a separate item in any cost-benefit analysis, since it will normally, because of price adjustments, be reflected in other parts of the equation. It is not, for example, necessary to count economies of scale achieved in the road services sector through the building of a motorway, if lower service prices have already been counted as part of the total benefit accruing to motorists.[43] But no such presumption can be made in the case of a command system. Since prices are fixed, there is no automatic mechanism whereby such benefits accrue to the original 'mover'. The planner in a command system must be as careful to avoid double-counting as his Western counterpart, but cannot rely on this kind of effect being internalized at the level of subordinate bodies. For our purposes, then, it appears as a genuine externality.

But can we use the term pecuniary externality in a command system? It is perhaps more accurate to talk of externally conditioned internal economies/diseconomies of scale. But this is really too clumsy, so let us settle for secondary agglomeration economies, while bearing in mind that this is not, in strict theory, a correct definition, since such economies could in fact be reaped in San Francisco as a result of some industrial development in Melbourne.

External production diseconomies, it has been said, exist because certain things – air, water, etc. – are free goods, or virtually free goods. It is important to note that for the Soviet Union we must, as far as subordinate organizations are concerned, include land among these free goods. As we have seen, land rent has never been charged in any systematic way in the Soviet Union. There has, of course, always been some tendency for all costs to be externalized – that is what the gross-output syndrome is partly about – but in the case of land there has usually been absolutely no constraint at all.

The particular way in which externalities problems may work out is obviously a function of the kind of organization involved. We would expect enterprises to be insensitive to production economies and diseconomies, and also secondary agglomeration economies, though neither case would be of great practical importance because of the limited degree of control of enterprises over investment funds. External economies of scale are by definition not relevant to enterprise decision-making. Ministries too can be expected to be insensitive to production economies/diseconomies, since they are unlikely to impinge on 'own' enterprises to any great extent. An excellent example of a production diseconomy on a scale which implicates intermediate body rather than enterprise is the pollution of the Caspian Sea by oil seepage of 65,000 tons per year from Baku, one of the major reasons why the sturgeon catch in the Caspian has been falling steadily.[44] Pollution has also been a big problem in Lake Baikal.[45] But the opposite problem – where the potential usefulness of by-products to other organizations is ignored – is also commonly found. One of the best known examples is timber offcuts. Reports indicate that these are often simply burnt for firewood or wasted, because of lack of subsidiary enterprises to make use of them.[46] It is obvious enough why timber procurement enterprises have little interest in the utilization of such by-products. But surely, the reader might think, a forestry ministry would count the chips? The interesting point is that the industry is so fragmented administratively, because of autarkical tendencies, that higher authority tends to be as narrow in its interests as the enterprise.[47] We have here, then, an instance of how the autarky phenomenon may indirectly exacerbate the externalities problem. Of course, in sectors where by-products pertain to a different sector no such complicating factors are necessary to produce an identical result. Wastage of gas extracted simultaneously with oil in the Volga/Urals region is a well-known example.[48] Another even more striking one is that of the Bratsk hydro-electric station. Here the 'by-product' was millions of tons of standing timber in the submersion zone. The project was run largely by the Ministries of Power and Power Construction, so that this colossal wastage of timber is hardly surprising.[49]

Ministries are obviously quite insensitive to external economies of scale of the transport variety. Indeed, as we have seen, their autarkical tendencies lead to excessive transport activity. With other externalities of this type they are content to reap without sowing, in this respect closely resembling the Western corporation – as long as we bear in mind that the Soviet ministry has always judged a particular economy or diseconomy primarily in terms of its relation to output performance. Thus they have been quite happy to enjoy the advantages of a skilled labour pool and a highly developed infrastructure in existing urban centres, but unwilling to contribute to the building-up of infrastructure and the labour force in less-developed regions. Since, however, they are concerned above all with output, the small 'unintegrated' plant on the periphery, contributing almost nothing to putative profitability, but a great deal to output through the supply of 'odds and ends', may, as far as the ministry is concerned, be quite happily located.

There is nothing very much to say about secondary agglomeration effects as far as ministries are concerned, except to emphasize that these organizations may be insensitive to the 'receiving' as well as to the 'giving out' of such bounties, inasmuch as they may not be particularly concerned about cost structures. But the more a given ministry has succeeded in building up a self-sufficient organization, the more it may, *ceteris paribus*, be concerned with the impact of such economies, as they are effectively internalized.

Now in principle one would expect a *sovnarkhoz* to be much more sensitive to externalities than a ministry or enterprise, simply because it is a spatially defined organization. Production externalities, external economies of scale and secondary agglomeration effects should all be taken in their stride by this kind of organization, always with the usual qualification in connection with the overriding orientation towards output. In fact, excessive smallness and badly drawn boundaries tended to vitiate this advantage just as they intensified the autarky problem. The case of Tyumen[1] oil shows that badly drawn boundaries can be quite enough on their own to cause problems with externalities. In addition, because of the land-rent anomaly, and because *sovnarkhozy* were not responsible for agriculture, extremely crude instances of a peculiarly Soviet type of production diseconomy can be cited from that period.

In choosing the site for the Tashkent GRES no thought whatsoever was given to the question of the routes for the high-tension transmission lines of 110 and 220 kilovolts. The problem received no clarification even in the *proekt* of the GRES, worked out by TashTEP. We must remember that there are 14 of these lines, and that they have to be laid through the densely populated territory of the Ordzhonikidze *raion*, with its big gardens, so that it will be necessary to dig up as much as 300 hectares of orchards. This can hardly be considered sensible.[50]

The process of investment in the Soviet system must, then, be seen in all its real complexity – complexity of motivation amongst policy-makers, complexity of problems at the implementation stage. Detailed discussion of the fascinating detail which makes up this complexity should not however be allowed to obscure the fundamental issues of growth strategy discussed in Chapter One, issues which have impinged on Soviet investment patterns more than anything, and which cannot simply be left in a little box entitled 'long-term economic considerations'. Nor should an account of the manifold difficulties and inefficiencies of the implementation process, and the many sins of the ministries, lead us to forget the great achievements of the Soviet Union in the field of regional policy, and in the quest for inter-regional economic equality.[51] But we are beginning to get on to a level of generalization which, if it is to be tolerated at all, is best left to a concluding chapter. In the meantime, we must complete the picture of the urban/industrial sector by looking at labour and its organization.

NOTES

1. 'Ob uluchshenii proektno – smetnogo dela', published in *Ekonomicheskaya Gazeta*, 26/69, pp. 12–13.
2. I. S. Zen'kov, M. Ya Rusakov, *Ekonomika Stroitel'stva, Vysshaya Shkola*, Moscow, 1967, p. 116; A. N. Grammatikov, *Ekonomicheskaya Reforma v Oblasti Planirovaniya, Finansirovaniya i Kreditovaniya Kapital'nykh Vlozhenii, Nedra*, Moscow, 1968, pp. 14–15.
3. 'Ob uluchsenii ...', p. 12.
4. For an excellent example, see A. Ferberg, 'O kapital'nykh vlozheniyakh na rekonstruktsiyu deistvuyushchikh pred-priyatii', in *Voprosy Ekonomiki*, 1/66, p. 118.
5. Grammatikov, *op. cit.*, pp. 14–17.
6. This impression was strongly confirmed in a conversation I had with a *Gosplan* Uzbekistan official in 1968.
7. Grammatikov, *op. cit.*, p. 58; V. Andarenko, 'Na poroge reformy v proektirovanii', in *Ekonomika Stroitel'stva*, 8/70, p. 12.

8. See I. Novikov, 'Proekt i stroika', in *Pravda*, 26 May 1974, p. 2.

9. G. Shiryaev, 'O sovershenstvovanii proektno-smetnogo dela', in *Planovoe Khozyaistvo*, 8/69, p. 58; O. Sitnikov, 'Tekhnicheskii progress i khozyaistvennaya reforma', in *Planovoe Khozyaistvo*, 9/69, p. 32.

10. See V. Krasovskii, *Problemy Ekonomiki Kapital'nykh Vlozhenii, Ekonomika*, Moscow, 1967, p. 45, for a discussion of the primitiveness of design techniques.

11. For an apposite comparison nearer home ask any academic how university departments, etc., operate in their efforts to ensure a maximum continuing flow of funds!

12. For examples, see Krasovskii, *op. cit.*, p. 46.

13. The construction side of the Cherepovets industrial area, for example, was covered by no less than thirty-nine design organizations! See ibid., p. 45.

14. Ibid., p. 47.

15. Note that in Soviet terminology construction is not counted as an industry in the narrow sense (*promyshlennost'*), but is given the title of *industriya*.

16. See contribution by V. S. Vainshtein to ed. T. S. Khachaturov, *Metody i Praktika Opredeleniya Effektivnosti Kapital'nykh Vlozhenii i Novoi Tekhniki, vypusk* 17, *Nauka*, Moscow, 1970, pp. 47–48.

17. Leader in *Izvestiya*, 13 March 1968; M. Odinets, 'Chto skryvaetsya za obshchimi slovami', in *Pravda*, 26 November 1968, p. 2.

18. For a fuller discussion of these points, see ed. P. D. Podshivalenko, *Ekonomika Stroitel'stva*, pp. 12–13.

19. See A. Bogatyrev, *et al.*, 'Dal'neishii shag po puti khozyaistvennoi reformy', in *Ekonomicheskaya Gazeta*, 23/75, p. 9.

20. E. Zolotnikov, L. Remezov, 'Novoe v pravilakh priemki v ekspluatatsiyu ob''ektov proizvodstvennogo naznacheniya', in *Ekonomika Stroitel'stva*, 5/66, pp. 28–29.

21. See I. Bakhtin, V. Bukhina, K. Ureevski, 'Predlozheniya, vytekayashchie iz praktiki', in *Ekonomika Stroitel'stva*, 3/65.

22. Lack of infrastructure on many big construction sites has meant that often only the more peripheral members of Soviet society have been prepared to work on them.

[94]

23. P. Shitenkov, 'K chemu provodyat proschety expertizy', in *Ekonomika Stroitel'stva*, 1/67, p. 49.

24. See ed. P. D. Podshivalenko and I. D. Sher, *Finansirovanie i Kreditovanie Kapital'nykh Vlozhenii*, 2nd ed., *Finansy*, Moscow, 1965, p. 61, on the effectiveness of *Stroibank* control at the *proekt* stage. For an example of a *vnutripostroechnyi titul'nyi spisok*, see ed. Podshivalenko, *Ekonomika Stroitel'stva*, pp. 106–110.

25. See Krasovskii, *op. cit.*, p. 50.

26. V. Isaev, 'Nekotorye voprosy khozyaistvennoi reformy i stroitel'stva', in *Voprosy Ekonomiki*, 5/70, p. 47.

27. In 1973 the volume of unfinished construction once again rose. See D. A. Dyker, 'The Soviet Economy in 1973', in *Soviet Analyst*, 14 February 1974.

28. On the Urals-Kuznetsk combine, see F. Holzman, 'The Soviet Ural-Kuznetsk combine', in *Quarterly Journal of Economics*, August 1957. On Bratsk, see ed. V. F. Mal'tsev, *Bratskaya GES. Sbornik Dokumentov i Materialov, Toma I and II, Vostochno-Sibirskoe Knizhnoe izdatel'stvo*, Irkutsk, 1964 and 1967.

29. See D. A. Dyker, 'Industrial location in the Tadzhik republic', in *Soviet Studies*, April, 1970.

30. See L. Ya. Feigin, 'Problemy razvitiya proizvoditel'nykh sil Sredneaziatskogo ekonomicheskogo raiona', in ed. N. N. Nekrasov, *Razvitie i Razmeshchenie Proizvoditel'nykh Sil Ekonomicheskikh Raionov SSSR, Nauka*, Moscow, 1967, p. 245.

31. For a detailed discussion of these principles, see I. S. Koropeckyj, 'The development of Soviet location theory before the Second World War' – I, in *Soviet Studies*, July 1967.

32. A recent *Pravda* report noted that the first stage of the new Oktyabr'skii copper mine in Noril'sk had been completed two years and three months ahead of schedule. The existence of 'technical problems' was, however, admitted. See *Pravda*, 3 April 1974.

33. For a detailed discussion see Dyker, 'Industrial location ...', *op. cit.*

34. See, for example, Yu. O. Alferov, G. Usmanov, E. N. Fatakhov, *Problemy Razvitiya Chernoi Metallurgii Srednei Azii, Fan*, Tashkent, 1971.

35. The author's visit to Tadzhikistan, and to the site of the dam

itself, in 1968, left him in no doubt of the pride taken in the project, whether in the Academy of Sciences, or on Main Street.

36. M. Mkrtchyan, 'Metodologicheskie voprosy razmeshcheniya proizvoditel¹nykh sil', in *Planovoe Khozyaistvo*, 12/69, p. 43.

37. G. I. Granik, *Ekonomicheskie Problemy Razvitiya i Razmeshcheniya Proizvoditel¹nykh Sil Evropeiskogo Severa SSSR, Nauka*, Moscow, 1971, p. 142.

38. See A. Nove, 'Soviet planning: reforms in prospect', in *Soviet Studies*, July 1962.

39. V. V. Kistanov, *Kompleksnoe Razvitie i Spetsializatsiya Ekonomicheskikh Raionov SSSR, Nauka*, Moscow, 1968, p. 191.

40. The reader should be assured that the author's originality in this section is purely terminological.

41. See A. Weber, *The Theory of the Location of Industries*, trans. C. J. Friedrich, University of Chicago Press, Chicago and London, 1929, Chapter V. Note, however, that under the agglomeration factor Weber included internal economies of scale, as long as they were of a locational nature.

42. See T. Scitovsky, 'Two concepts of external economies', in eds. A. N. Agarwala and S. P. Singh, *The Economics of Underdevelopment*, Oxford University Press, Bombay, 1958.

43. See A. R. Prest and R. Turvy, 'Cost-benefit analysis: a survey', in *Surveys of Economic Theory*, Vol. 3, Macmillan, London, 1966, pp. 161–162.

44. See A. Iordanskii, 'Kaspii zovet na pomoshch¹', in *Khimiya i Zhizn¹*, 1/70, pp. 51–52.

45. See M. I. Goldman, *The Spoils of Progress: Environmental Pollution in the Soviet Union*, M.I.T. Press, Cambridge, Mass., and London, 1972, Chapter 6.

46. See Ye. Ligachev, 'Effektivnee ispol¹zovat¹ bogatstva zapadnosibirskoi nizmennosti', in *Ekonomicheskaya Gazeta*, 8/68, p. 6.

47. See A. Zheludkov, 'Krupnyi rezerv ekonomii', in *Planovoe Khozyaistvo*, 8/66, especially p. 22.

48. See ed. A. A. Adamesku, *Problemy Razvitiya i Razmeshcheniya Proizvoditel¹nykh Sil Povol¹zha, Mysl¹*, Moscow, 1973, pp. 95–97.

49. See Mal¹tsev, *op. cit.*

50. K. Abrosimova, 'Raionnye planirovki i razmeshchenie

promyshlennosti', in *Narodnoe Khozyaistvo Uzbekistana*, 12/60, pp. 13–14.

51. Significant differences in levels of national income per head between regions do, of course, still exist. See L. N. Talepko, *Urovni Ekonomicheskogo Razvitiya Raionov SSSR*, *Ekonomika*, Moscow, 1971.

CHAPTER SIX

Labour and its Organization in the non-Agricultural Sector

Too often labour is stuck away in a chapter by itself in textbooks on the Soviet economy, and the present work, the author fears, is no exception. But conscience can be salved to some extent by emphasizing, right from the start, that 'labour' is not a separate sector of the economy in the way that 'agriculture' is, but a dimension of the subject to which the last three chapters have been devoted – the organization of industrial and service economic activity. The merit of the present arrangement is its convenience, not its logic.

The early history of Soviet labour, or rather of the Soviet trade union movement, is fascinating, inasmuch as it includes the famous episode of the 'workers' opposition'. But this belongs to political rather than to economic history.[1] The outstanding characteristics of the labour situation in the 1920s, for present purposes, were as follows:

1. There was a serious unemployment problem. In 1928 unemployment in the non-agricultural sector was running at around 11 per cent.[2]

2. Unemployment benefit existed, in addition to a number of other social benefits.[3]

3. The trade unions occupied a somewhat ambivalent position. They were certainly not independent of the government, but did maintain some degree of autonomy *vis-à-vis* it.[4]

4. Wage rates were officially centrally controlled, but in practice wages tended to be determined on the basis of local collective bargaining.[5]

As with everything else, radical changes supervened in the labour field in the late 1920s and 1930s. The unions were reduced to the status of 'hurrah' organizations, concerned with what the state could get out of the workers, rather than vice versa.[6] Central control over wage rates was positively asserted, though not necessarily, as we shall see, to the exclusion of elements of *de facto* decentralization as far as actual wage payments are concerned. Unemployment benefit was abolished in 1930, along with the 'abolition' of unemployment.[7] The initiation of the great industrialization drive did in fact ensure that a situation of marked labour shortage became prevalent.

Even under 'full Stalinism' there was, however, never any question of subjecting the supply of labour to systematic direct control. It is, indeed, this characteristic which distinguishes the labour 'market' from most other 'markets' in the Soviet economy. This is not to say that important elements of direct control have not been present at various times. Legislation passed in 1940–42 deprived workers of the right to change jobs without permission, and made provision for direction of labour. About the same time the so-called labour reserve schools, effectively a means of directing young people into particular occupations, were created. These provisions, however, fell largely out of use long before their official repeal in 1956.[8] Of more lasting importance has been the power of direction over Party members, and over graduates of higher educational institutions for the first three years after graduation.

The membership of the Communist Party of the Soviet Union includes the vast bulk of the Soviet élite. Membership of the Party is voluntary, but the point is that resignation from the Party is tantamount to renouncing membership of the élite, and anyone taking such a step would thenceforth be regarded as politically unreliable, and therefore unfit for any kind of high office. There can be no doubt, then, about the importance of the Party regulation.

The existence of the legal power of graduate direction does not, of course, mean that every graduate is, in fact, directed. More important, graduate direction has not always been a tremendously effective instrument. Particular difficulties have been encountered in trying to ensure that personnel directed to some of the more isolated parts of the Soviet Union actually get there. A recent

Izvestiya report complained that engineers assigned to *Kalugasel'stroi* (Moscow region) from Nal'chik (North Caucasus region) had continued to live, and in one case to work, in local government service in Nal'chik[9] – this despite the fact that (a) graduates stand to lose their diploma if they fail to comply with their instructions, and (b) it is illegal for any other than their 'proper' enterprise to employ them.[10] It is, furthermore, clear that graduates with good *blat*, either directly or through relatives, may be able to arrange allocation to a desirable area and job.[11] Quite apart from nepotism, good graduates do, understandably, tend to get the pick of the jobs going.[12] But perhaps a more serious problem than the one of enforceability is that of the efficiency of direction of graduates. A *cause célèbre* of a few years ago illustrates the kind of problems that can arise. Faina Konovalova, a graduate in heat technology of the Kuibyshev Politechnic Institute, was directed, in accordance with the regulations, to the Omsk oil processing plant. On arrival she quickly discovered that the plant did not need a heating engineer, and indeed had not asked for one. She was offered various alternative jobs, including a factory floor one, and was on occasion assigned wholly fictitious duties. When vacancies for engineering posts arose she was by-passed. Her requests to be allowed to seek alternative employment were, however, turned down. After two years she wrote to *Komsomol'skaya Pravda*. All this took place in a situation of overall shortage of graduate manpower at the enterprise.[13] The rector of the Kuibyshev Institute confirmed that cases of this nature were common.[14]

Clearly, if neither state nor personal interests are served by a given decision, the value of the institution in any terms must be open to question. More specifically, a question mark is raised over the whole issue of job information – to planners as well as job-seekers. We shall return to this point presently.

In addition to these principal forms of direction, there is the system of passport and police registration regulations, which has been used fairly widely as a means of limiting labour flows into the big conurbations, especially Moscow. This sort of approach has also been used to a limited extent to try to limit population flows to the fashionable areas of the south – most notoriously, to prevent the Crimean Tartars, deported *en masse* in 1941 and rehabilitated in 1967, from actually returning to their homeland, no doubt with no more sinister motive than to prevent over-population of that desirable peninsula.[15]

In the late 1930s and early 1940s there was of course a heavy incidence of crude slave labour. Both the quantitative extent of forced labour following the purges of 1937–38 and the precise motivation on the part of Stalin remain a subject of controversy. Estimates of the peak number of inmates of forced labour camps vary between 7 and 12 million.[16] The purges were obviously very much to do with Stalin's dictatorial, and possibly paranoid temperament, and arguably with the whole logic of the institutional system which emerged from the industrialization drive. What is not altogether clear is whether we can find a conscious economic motive in the phenomenon. It is certainly true that the NKVD (National Commissariat for Internal Affairs) came to control a very high percentage of Soviet national income in that period.[17] It is probable that 'plans' were sometimes issued for arrests,[18] which may seem to suggest some motive beyond the purely political, though it may equally well simply reflect the logic of an institutional system.[19] Common sense would point to the conclusion that the basic attitude was that personnel, once arrested, might as well be used, rather than that they were arrested in order that they might be used. Whatever one's opinion on this controversial point might be, however, it is undeniable that a number of the great projects of the 1930s, implemented as they were often in the most inhospitable climates and with the barest minimum of infrastructure, would probably never have been completed without forced labour. The White Sea canal is an outstanding example.[20] On the other hand, it is important to bear in mind the enormous administrative costs of the system as a whole, and it must remain doubtful whether this episode in Soviet economic history was on balance 'economical', even if the broader implications of the period of purges for general economic efficiency are ignored.[21]

Beyond the clearly defined elements of direct control over labour supply we find institutions and roles which lie in a rather shadowy territory in between helping labour to make up its own mind, and actually making up labour's mind for it. In the 1930s *orgnabor* (short for *organizovannyi nabor* – organized recruitment) was the institution which emerged as being centrally concerned with the transferral of rural working population into the growing urban/industrial centres. The evidence does not suggest, however, that much that could be described as outright coercion took place in this work. Quotas were established for *kolkhozy*, but

> individual *kolkhoz* members had somewhat more freedom of movement, on paper as well as in fact. As the number of workers to be recruited by industry was invariably limited in comparison with total *kolkhoz* membership, the quotas could often be met without resorting to compulsion ...[22]

After the war *orgnabor* switched over largely to the task of organizing the transfer of labour out to the eastern parts of the Soviet Union. In this, however, it has enjoyed fairly limited success, partly for reasons connected with wage differentials, as we shall see later, but also through poor organization.[23] There has, indeed, been a tendency for the *Komsomol* (Communist Youth League) to take over this role from *orgnabor*. The classic example is the '*Komsomol* call-up' (*komsomol'skii prizyv*) which provided a large part of the workforce for the 'Virgin Lands' scheme, which we will be discussing in the next chapter. The role of the *Komsomol* in galvanizing youth labour remains important to the present day. The recently commenced Baikal-Amur railway line, for instance, has been declared an 'all-union *Komsomol* crash project'.[24] There can be little doubt that *Komsomol* operations in the labour placement field may often border on 'volunteering' of the traditional British army type.[25] But there can be no question of elements of crude coercion being present to any significant extent.

If direct control has been of essentially marginal importance, what are the principal ways in which the Soviet authorities try to influence the distribution of labour? Two main instruments of indirect control are, in fact, used – the educational system and the wage system.

The Soviet educational system is a subject in itself, and we must limit ourselves here to a discussion of the system as a means whereby the state can influence the 'assortment' of trainings and specialities that come on the market. In doing this we must, however, bear in mind Nigel Grant's dictum that

> the aim of the Soviet authorities has always been the building of a new kind of society, and they have used the educational system,

deliberately and consciously, as a means of attaining this goal. It is, therefore, designed not merely as a machine for the production of scientists, engineers and technicians, but as an instrument of mass education from which the younger generation gain not only their formal learning, but their social, moral, and political ideas as well.[26]

Educational planning – the number of places made available for the study of different subjects at higher education institutions, etc., does, nevertheless, take account of the needs of the economy in a more comprehensive way than we are used to in the West.

What are the practical implications of this general policy orientation? In particular, how may it affect the individual pupil or student? We have already discussed the provisions for direction of graduates. In addition, there is plenty of evidence that the Soviet authorities are prepared to apply pressure on young people as they make their career choices. An extreme case was reported in *Pravda* in 1968. A school-leaver in Zdolbunov wanted to go into the construction industry. At first all seemed to be going smoothly, but trouble started when the boy was refused the necessary confirmation by the vice-chairman of the *raion* executive committee. An interview between the boy's father and the vice-chairman elicited the explanation that School No. 4 was permitted to place its graduates only at railway depots. The father wrote to *Pravda*, and the newspaper got in touch with the vice-chairman, and it was eventually established that the boy could, in fact, be a construction worker if he so wished.[27]

To repeat, this is an extreme case – after all, it was reported with disapproval and censure – but it indicates how, in a climate where it is accepted that the state has a legitimate right to be concerned about career choices, persuasion may ease into coercion, particularly, one supposes, when harassed local officials are searching for solutions to short-term economic problems.

For all this the Soviet educational system remains fairly conservatively academic in its approach to curricula. The idea of polytechnicization (*politekhnizatsiya*), whereby schoolchildren mix academic with practical work, has been much discussed and publicized in the Soviet Union, but implementation has been limited. Khrushchev's 1958 reform placed heavy emphasis on the polytechnical ideal, with schoolchildren being sent out for work sessions at neighbourhood factories. The motivation behind this campaign was complex. Ideological considerations were mixed up with a concern to increase the supply of blue-collar labour, and to reduce pressure on places in higher education. But severe practical difficulties were encountered in the implementation of these schemes, and the basic emphasis in Soviet schools today remains on a traditional approach centred on classroom and teacher.[28]

For those not going on to higher education the crucial stage of specialization comes after the completion of the basic seven or eight years of compulsory education. (The extra year is a peculiarity of the Baltic republics.) Various institutions exist, such as secondary specialized schools (*srednic spetsial'nye uchebnye zavedeniya*), and vocational-technical schools (*professional'no-tekhnicheskie uchilishcha* – the successors to the old labour reserve schools), which provide the kind of training a British adolescent would normally receive under an apprenticeship/day release scheme.

Though it is not impossible to proceed from the abovementioned types of school to a higher educational institution, the normal route is through the ten- or eleven-year middle school, or rather the extra three years of that school. At the end of the tenth or eleventh year pupils may take the certificate of fitness (*attestat zrelosti*), roughly equivalent to the GCE, which is the basis for entry into a VUZ (*vysshee uchebnoe zavedenie* – higher educational institution). All potential entrants into higher education must however also pass an entrance examination for the particular institution they wish to enter.

Apart from these principal types of school, there are certain special types. The ones which are of particular importance in the present context are those for the artistically gifted, and for pupils of outstanding promise in mathematics and certain other subjects. These institutions are quite explicitly orientated to the segregation and development of the pupil with flair. They involve only a small percentage of children, however, and modify to no serious extent the basic comprehensive, non-streamed orientation of Soviet school education.

There are many different types of VUZ – the specialized institute plays a much greater role in Soviet than it does in British higher education. Only arts and theoretical science subjects are taught in the universities. Beyond these there are technical institutes, agricultural institutes, 'institutes of national economy' producing applied economists and accountants, medical institutes, etc. Teaching in VUZy is largely through lectures, while assessment takes the form principally of oral examinations, with 'original work' a relatively minor item. Graduates of VUZy receive a diploma, and may proceed to study for the degree of *kandidat* – a research degree with a somewhat lower status than the British or American Ph.D. The *doktorat* is a degree to which only outstanding academics can aspire.

It is clear that the structure of Soviet education is basically conventionally academic – though on continental rather than Anglo-Saxon lines. We should not, then, make the mistake of envisaging a system which integrates education directly into the working life of the community. There is scope for the integration of long-term production and educational plans, and for elements of informal compulsion in career choice. It is certainly considered perfectly normal that social pressure should be applied to individuals to go in particular career directions. But in many cases of shortage of particular kinds of labour the authorities have been unable or unwilling to use this scope decisively. One is, indeed, tempted to speculate that the principal way in which the Soviet education system contributes to control over labour supply is at the general psychological level. Conservative teaching techniques, an assessment system which gives very little encouragement to original work, and a fairly tight hierarchical relationship between different levels, may combine to produce a fairly docile average *vypusknik*. But at the level of the particular the role of the educational system should not be exaggerated.

Turning now to the wage system, we are confronted with a picture which is nothing if not complex. Basic rates in particular industries normally vary in accordance with a seven-category classification of degree of skill on the part of the worker. Straight time work is varied by individual and group piecework. Special rates are fixed for workers in remote and/or inhospitable areas. So detailed are the wage regulations, indeed, that the sheer accounting problem of making sure that the official rates are observed must be immense. But there are other, more systematic, reasons why wage control is less complete in practice than in principle.

We must refer back to the general issue of cost constraints.

Under the classical system, and to some extent even now, the success-indicator regime tended to militate against careful observation of such constraints, and even to create direct incentives to their violation. Labour costs are a major element in total costs, so we can expect, *a priori*, a tendency for wage plans to be violated. The piecework and grading systems create scope for 'avoidance' as opposed to 'evasion' of control. Workers are commonly upgraded simply as a strategem for giving them a wage rise. Piecework norms are often overfulfilled by over 50 per cent, and recent efforts to introduce a greater degree of meaningfulness into norms, under the rubric of NOT (*nauchnaya organizatsiya truda* – scientific organization of labour) have met with only limited success.[29] This kind of situation is of course perfectly familiar to the student of piecework systems in the West,[30] but its significance is much greater in a system where comprehensive control over wage payments is sought. Scope for systematic manoeuvring within the payment regulations is limited by control of the aggregate wage fund, but this control is clearly only partially effective. We can, then, talk of a *sui generis* type of cost-push inflation, which may be of crucial importance in understanding movements in the level of repressed inflation, and indeed in the level of prices on the *kolkhoz* market.[31] If we move into the sphere of violation of explicit regulations, we can find quite extraordinary examples of excess payment to labour.

> Usually the foreman goes around the building site the day before the day-off and seductively rustles money in his pocket. He offers five, ten, even twenty rubles to anyone willing to turn out for work on his law-given rest day. Some agree, but as a rule few take the money home. They drink it all away. What good is this to anyone?[32]

To put this into perspective, the average basic weekly wage of a building worker around 1970 was in the region of 30–35 roubles.

Wage payments do, then, to some extent fluctuate despite central control and understandably the fluctuations tend to reflect the supply and demand situation as perceived at enterprise level, though they may also reflect simply the exigencies of a given success-indicator situation. There is in other words a kind of market for labour which operates quite independently of central plans, though not of course necessarily against the spirit of those plans. Enterprises do in fact compete for labour, and to complete the picture it is important to emphasize that non-wage benefits, particularly housing, can be just as important here as money payments. This point is illustrated with typical Crocodilian humour in Fig. 3.

Fig. 3 The scene is at the door of the personnel department of an unnamed factory. Workers are queueing with 'requests to be relieved of duties' in their hands. 'What's going?' 'Housing.' 'But where?' 'At the factory down the road.' (*Krokodil*, 10/69, p. 4. Drawing by A. Grunin)

When all is said and done however, the Soviet authorities do effectively exercise a degree of control over real wage payments far in excess of what is possible for a Western government. But how efficiently do they utilize this power?

There can be no doubt that through differentials and bonus schemes of various kinds the Soviet authorities have, to a considerable extent, succeeded in conditioning the workforce to central priorities. We have already noted the crucial role of managerial bonus payments, while recognizing the important respects in which the system of incentives produces perverse results. Basic priorities on the relative importance of different industries have been effectively emphasized through the wage system. However much the relatively poor remuneration of service and retail workers has contributed to the demoralization of these workers, and indirectly to the suffering of the Soviet consumer,[33] it has helped to keep the system heavy-industry orientated. Where the wage system has been much less effective is in regulating inter-regional labour flows in accordance with state plans.

Perhaps the most telling statistic on this point is the net outflow of population from Siberia over the period 1956–60. Indeed, over the much longer period 1939–59 immigration into Siberia only just matched emigration – and this despite all the efforts of *orgnabor*, the *Komsomol*, etc.[34] To take a more specific instance, between 1960 and 1967, 152,446 people arrived at Vorkuta, in the European far north, and 152,751 left.[35] Why so? After making allowances for poor quality labour-placement work, conditioned inevitably by orientation towards quantitative success-indicators,[36] one would naturally seek for an answer in terms of the inadequacy of the established extra payments in making up for austere climate, remote location, and infrastructural poverty. The reality, however, has been somewhat starker. The basic problem has been quite simply that the extra wage payments have been inadequate to compensate for the extra expense of living, in terms of higher food prices, greater expenditure on clothing and heating, etc., so that even on a straightforward calculation families resident in the outlying areas have often been worse off than families resident in the metropolitan and southern areas. A 1966 calculation, for example, showed that the cost of living in Eastern Siberia was 20 per cent above that of the Central region, while wages were only 18 per cent higher.[37] A decree of 1967 improved the take-home pay position of workers in the north and far east, but it remains to be seen whether this will have any significant effect.[38]

The general demographic trend in the Soviet Union in the postwar period has been a drift from north to south. The Ukraine, Transcaucasia, North Caucasus, Kazakhstan and Central Asia have been the areas enjoying the highest rate of net immigration,[39] and attempts by the authorities to bring these tendencies under control have not met with a great deal of success. This does not necessarily imply that purely 'arithmetic' anomalies of the kind just discussed have occurred systematically. It is equally probable that the quest for sun and a Mediterranean life style is just as strong in the Soviet Union as elsewhere, and as difficult to control through purely financial measures. It should in any case be borne in mind that no system of control of labour movement can possibly effect meaningful control if the production side of the economy is not also under meaningful control. In the case of the big con-urbations, particularly Moscow, attempts to prevent the ministries from continuing expansion of basic capacities in these locations have been singularly unsuccessful, as we saw in Chapter Five. Clearly, once a job is created, however much against the wishes of the central authorities, it has to be filled in one way or another. One is left speculating how much the ministries have been able to affect national labour policies from inside, as it were, as opposed to simply evading them.

At the macro-economic level, then, wage policy has been of considerable importance in inter-sectoral terms, but fairly ineffectual in inter-regional terms. This latter point does, by the way, throw considerable light on some of the surviving elements of direct control discussed earlier. If we try to come down to the question of how well the wage system ensures that a given in-dividual worker finds himself in a work situation which adequately balances his own preferences and the needs of the state, as expressed through the money wage, we are obviously faced with considerable problems of information. Some indication can be gained, however, through the study of particular phenomena, characteristic of the Soviet labour scene. One that has been well documented is *tekuchest*[1].

Tekuchest[1] literally means simply mobility. The implication, however, is of excessive mobility. Perhaps this indicates a tend-ency amongst the Soviets to see any degree of mobility as being in some sense undesirable, possibly as a hangover from wartime. In fact, however, the rate of turnover of labour in many Soviet factories is often very high by any standards. Cases where more than 50 per cent of the labour force has left in the course of a single year are common. In particular instances the picture is even more striking. In 1971, for example, the Kustanai furniture factory (Kazakhstan) had a rate of turnover of 93 per cent.[40] How much direct 'wastage' has this involved? A 1966 survey gave seventeen and twenty-three days as the average period between jobs in, respectively, Moscow and Leningrad.[41] A survey done in Dushanbe, the capital of Tadzhikistan, in 1968–69 came up with a figure of thirty-two days.[42] It is not surprising, then, that high rates of *tekuchest*[1] have been reflected in fairly high rates of frictional unemployment.

What lies behind the *tekuchest*[1] problem? This must remain to some extent a controversial point, at least as far as relative emphasis is concerned. But a number of general observations can be made with confidence. It is clear that *de facto* autonomous determination of wages at grass-roots level does create differentials which induce 'flitting', and which may be consciously aimed at 'stealing' labour. Reference back to Figure 3 will remind us that it may be amenities rather than money wages which are the crucial variable. It is furthermore clear, particularly in the case of the construction industry, that the poor living conditions and almost complete lack of infrastructure which workers may have to put up with creates, or rather reinforces, an orientation towards a semi-hobo way of life which is anything but conducive to stability of workplace.[43] Lastly, *tekuchest*[1] may be partly an expression of general dissatisfaction or, if you like, of 'alienation', on the part of the Soviet worker.[44]

To return to the question of *de facto* competition for labour: one notes that in Western countries, where such competition is much less trammelled, large-scale 'flitting' is not induced, because major variations in net benefits of what might be termed a windfall variety simply do not emerge. This is obviously partly due to the homogenizing influence of the trade unions. But it is due also to the simple fact that the forces of competition tend to lead to the obviation of anomalies and the imposition of uniformity. The point about the Soviet situation is, firstly, that the extent of 'freedom' is not uniform between enterprises – it varies depending on the *blat* of the director, the wiliness of the chief accountant, the priority of the job being done, etc.; secondly, that one of the primary requisites of effective competition – namely adequate information – has been to a great extent lacking in the Soviet case. When unemployment was officially 'abolished' in the USSR, so were labour exchanges.[45] Perhaps this reflected a prejudice with which we are quite familiar in the UK – namely that labour exchanges are places which try to find work for men actually unemployed, rather than trying to find more suitable jobs for men already employed, i.e. being genuinely concerned with the allocation of labour. In any case, the result of this was that for many years information on job opportunities was limited to occasional press or radio announcements, or even just a poster stuck on a telegraph pole. Inadequate informational services may have had two effects in connection with *tekuchest*[1]. Firstly, it must clearly be an inducement to wander around from one plant to another in search of the 'right' job. Secondly, it must permit anomalies to survive because they cannot easily become known. What is, of course, known is that anomalies exist, if only they can be found!

There have always been some organizations of the labour exchange type in operation. *Orgnabor* is partly that, but has always had a restricted remit, and has in any case not been very efficient. More recently 'labour-placement' (*trudoustroistvo*) has been attracting more systematic attention. Republican committees for the utilization of labour resources were created in 1967. This was followed almost immediately by the creation of a *sluzhba truda* (labour service) network in the RSFSR, operating throughout the republic, and handling 240,000 workers in 1967, 400,000 in 1968, and over a million in 1970.[46] It is worth noting that the RSFSR network has also been entrusted with *orgnabor* work, and that labour-placement organizations are being created in other republics. A bureau of information and employment was created in Tadzhikistan in 1971, for example, with bureaux in the major cities of Kazakhstan appearing in the following year.[47] There does not, however, appear to be any kind of Union-wide organization to integrate the activities of these republican services, and this must be a serious obstacle to efficiency, especially where inter-regional labour movements are concerned. Another problem that has arisen indicates the difficulty with which old dogs are taught this particular new trick. A recent report from

Odessa states that the local bureau was restricting information to those already actually out of work, as a way of reducing *tekuchest'*![48]

Nevertheless, the new bureaux have undoubtedly enjoyed a considerable measure of success. *Sluzhba truda* has apparently reduced the average time between jobs to ten to sixteen days,[49] and in particular instances the reduction may have been even greater. The importance of this in the light of the incidence of *tekuchest'* is clear enough, and must surely grow to the extent that the so-called Shchekino experiment is extended throughout the Soviet Union.

In 1967 the Shchekino Chemical Combine (Tula *oblast'*) was conceded a right which no Soviet enterprise had enjoyed since NEP. Management would be permitted to make workers redundant without necessarily finding them alternative employment and to use the funds released in this way for general incentive purposes.[50] Vague statements had been made in 1965 about increasing managerial rights in this area, but the Soviet tradition has always placed heavy emphasis on security of employment on the part of the worker. The Shchekino experiment does, then, represent a radical departure, and reflects increasing concern on the part of the Soviet leadership with raising labour productivity through the excision of underemployment and a more rational allocation of labour resources. In October 1969 the Central Committee of the Communist Party did, in fact, pass a decree recommending the Shchekino model to all party workers.[51] The experiment has since been extended to other enterprises, but is still a long way from becoming the rule – at the beginning of 1971 just 121 enterprises were on the experimental system,[52] and these were probably predominantly dynamic and expanding organizations, able to a great extent to reabsorb labour surpluses internally. More recent reports indicate no dramatic expansion of this number. Clearly the leadership is treating the matter with caution, and with some reason. According to the best available Western estimate the rate of unemployment in the Soviet Union is not negligible – 1·3 per cent by American definitions.[53] This unemployment is largely frictional – see our earlier discussion of *tekuchest'*. But too much Shchekino without enough *trudoustroistvo* could raise the figure to a politically unacceptable level, and it must surely be a primary condition of any generalization of the

Shchekino system that an efficient nationwide network of labour-placement organizations should be set up.

We have been rather discourteous to the trade unions by leaving discussion of their fate since the 1920s to such a late stage in the chapter, but this may perhaps be to some extent a justified reflection of their fairly minor role, at least as trade unions in the Western sense.

The structure of Soviet trade unions (the Russian word is *profsoyuzy* – short for *professional'nye soyuzy* – literally professional unions) is uniformly industrial. Everyone from director to charlady is a member. Membership is not actually compulsory, but non-membership involves the loss of many amenity rights – housing, holiday camps, and even social insurance.[54] The central union organization is the All-Union Central Council of Trade Unions (AUCCTU). The grass-roots organization of the unions is based on factory union committees and their secretaries.

What is the role of Soviet trade unions? To repeat what was said earlier, their basic job in the Stalin period was to galvanize the workers. They did, and still do, organize so-called 'socialist competition' (*sotsialisticheskoe sorevnovanie*) – production figure contests between enterprises. These may have been used to some extent as a means of introducing a greater degree of flexibility into the plan implementation system (see discussion of problems of achieving balance in Chapter Two), and indeed involve some degree of material incentive. Basically, however, they have operated as a basis for the development of 'moral stimulation', and it is interesting that at the present time, despite the emphasis of the reformed system on material incentives, socialist competition seems to be receiving a new emphasis in the Soviet press.[55] A phenomenon peculiar to the late 1930s, and organized by the unions, was the famous Stakhanovite movement, a kind of ultra-extreme form of Taylorist piecework system, though including pure 'hurrah' elements.[56] Over and above this, the union organizational hierarchy has administered social security, thus effectively fulfilling the role of Ministry of Labour. On paper they have also had the task of protecting workers, and of seeing that they are justly treated, in terms of grading, bonus payments, etc. But how real has this last role been?

Up to the middle 1950s probably not very real at all. As E. C.

Brown, author of the standard work on the subject, has said of the position in the late 1930s:

> ... the unions in the plants were chiefly occupied with propaganda and efforts to increase production. They shared in settling grievances, administered disability benefits and other welfare services, and carried on cultural and educational activities; but there was widespread feeling among workers that the unions were chiefly agencies of management and the party, not able or willing to do much for their members.[57]

The post-Stalin era does, however, seem to have brought some kind of development in the role of the trade unions, and a movement from pseudo-ambivalence to a more genuine ambivalence. AUCCTU continues to operate as a ministry of labour, shop-floor organizations continue to fulfil the 'hurrah' function and the trade union committee chairman remains an active 'collaborator' with management. But at the same time union organizations have increasingly given their official role as protectors of labour a greater degree of content. This is particularly true with respect to working conditions, etc., but applies also to questions of grading, payment of bonuses, etc. One union committee chairman interviewed by Brown

> ... said, clenching his fist, 'This union is strong and brave.' He went on to say, 'Whether there is a dispute depends on the director. A clever director never has a dispute with the workers. If he can convince us, the committee accepts his opinion. But this plant committee is able to settle questions itself; it has no need for outside help.'[58]

It is important, however, not to exaggerate the extent to which the unions have reformed. Reports of domination of union committees by managerial personnel, inactivity or impotence in the face of infringement of safety regulations, illegal dismissal, illegal overtime, etc., have continued through the 1960s into the 1970s.[59] In 1973 a Sverdlovsk metallurgy worker complained of enterprise managements and trade union committees making agreements between themselves on socialist competitions without consulting the workers![60] As usual, however, it is important to place such phenomena in the context of what we have seen of the general operation of the Soviet economy. A manager who is forced by the success-indicator situation to resort to *shturmov-*

shchina is bound to become involved in infringement of overtime regulations, and probably also of regulations on working conditions. And with a lot of 'fast' roubles flying around there can be no presumption that every worker is primarily concerned with his legal rights.

What of the primary role of unions, as conceived in the West, namely negotiation over wage rates? It is open to anyone to speculate that, in an increasingly pluralistic Soviet political system, the national union leaders could, if they wanted to, exert pressure to raise general wage levels, subject of course to the constraint of defence priorities, with all their ramifications in terms of investment and heavy industry. But it is quite impossible to get any information on this, so that it must remain at the level of pure speculation. What may likewise be speculatively suggested, but with more circumstantial evidence to back it up, is that, given the undoubted fact of the existence of a certain amount of un-official wage bargaining at plant level, and given that the unions do seem to have adopted a much more positive role on many matters, including grading and bonuses, two and two could be put together to make a local union organization which is prepared to bargain with the director, on behalf of the workers, on total emoluments. After all, the union committee chairman is in a position to 'shop' the director on any legal and semi-legal man-oeuvre of the type often involved on the *de facto* labour market. Might not the apparent derelictions of the union organizations, as documented in the last paragraph, perhaps be the other side of a coin which very adequately expresses the truly felt needs of the workers – namely for more money, one way or the other? Unfortunately the range of the Soviet press does not give us an opportunity to bring direct evidence to bear on this hypothesis.

Before closing this chapter it is worth making a few observations about the special place of women within the Soviet labour force. The rate of female participation is high – something like 70 per cent of adult women are in employment. This reflects government policy – both on equality of the sexes and on utiliza-tion of the potential labour force – but it also reflects the difficulty in the Soviet Union of achieving a decent urban family standard of living on the basis of only one income. Back-up policies on kindergartens, etc., have been perhaps more effectively imple-mented than in most countries, though with some unevenness, and a serious neglect of rural areas.[61] But female employment policy has, intentionally or otherwise, sometimes rather neglected the non-work needs of the ladies involved, and, by implication, those of male workers also.

> The Kamyshin textile giant was built four times bigger than the norm for large-scale weaving establishments. It was argued that this yielded economies in terms of use of generating capacity and other subsidiary activities, but the problems posed by the creation of a demand for female labour in excess of local supply were ignored. Workers (i.e. female workers – D.A.D.) coming in from elsewhere find a strong preponderance of females, and this leads to a high rate of *tekuchest*[1].[62]

Clearly the prospect of a better job may not be the only reason for going on the road!

More serious, however, has been a tendency for some of the traditional difficulties of female employment to persist. Though female directors are not unknown they are uncommon, and only one woman has ever made it to the *Politburo*.[63] Traditionally male-dominated sectors like the coal industry do have their female representatives, but again they are rare. The latter fact is perhaps of limited importance. Equality of the sexes presumably does not necessarily mean unisex. But the low representation of women in the upper reaches generally does pinpoint a serious problem. While no doubt male prejudice in middle hierarchies may provide a partial explanation, we have no reason to doubt the sincerity and consistency of central policies here. The trouble is, of course, that as long as traditional family life survives in any form, no matter how comprehensive a system of home and family services there is, women will have less emotional energy, whatever their 'true' ambitions, to devote to the question of promotion, and, given the basic facts of childbearing, will remain, with the best will in the world, less suitable candidates for promotion.

A problem which seems at first glance less easy to explain in such fundamental terms is the fact that the preponderance of women in low-paid professions, like the retail trade, agriculture, teaching and medicine, has tended to neutralize official policies on equal pay. One could of course be cynical here, and simply attribute the fact to the 'real' policy of the central authorities. If this explanation is rejected, it is difficult to avoid the conclusion that the basic supply and demand situation must in some way be the key. Are women indeed suitable for only a limited range of jobs, so that in a situation of mass female employment there is an excess supply of labour in these sectors, or at least a lack of opportunity to force the hands of the authorities by changing jobs? If we do go for a supply and demand explanation, however, it is worth noting that we may still end up with childbearing as the ultimate explanation. It would seem that the kinds of job apparently favoured by Soviet women are in general those little involved with industrial technology, and so more suitable for a career which is going to be interrupted by pregnancy, etc. But it is very difficult to know just how much importance should be attached to this point. One argument sometimes advanced suggests that women are only concerned with making 'pin-money', and are therefore not concerned to maximize their earnings to the same extent as men. Whether or not this argument is applicable anywhere, it certainly seems quite inappropriate for the Soviet Union.[64]

It is not easy to find meaningful generalizations with which to close a chapter on Soviet labour, if only because so much that is of basic importance is still in a transitional stage. What does emerge, however, is that the labour 'market' is the great anomaly in the Soviet command system, in theory and more so in practice. On the other hand, we must not forget the still far from negligible elements of direct control and informal pressurization in the system. Nor should we forget that everything proceeds against the background of the Soviet political and security system so that, for instance, the most usual 'ultimate weapon' of the worker in the West, namely the strike, is used only at great risk, including risk of bodily harm.[65] Nevertheless, if experimental changes of the Shchekino variety continue and are extended, then change in the labour situation may go further and faster than changes in the production planning situation.

NOTES

1. See E. H. Carr, *The Bolshevik Revolution 1917-23*, Vol. I, Macmillan, London, 1950, pp. 203-208.
2. J. Chapman, *Real Wages in Soviet Russia since 1928*, Harvard University Press, Cambridge, Mass., 1963, p. 167.
3. See Gladkov, *op. cit.*, pp. 539-545.

4. See E. H. Carr, *The Interregnum 1923–1924*, London, 1954, pp. 51–54; *Socialism in One Country*, Vol. I, Macmillan, London, 1958, pp. 417–430.
5. See Nove, *An Economic History of the USSR*, p. 116.
6. See S. M. Schwarz, *Labor in the Soviet Union*, Cresset Press, London, 1953, Chapter 6.
7. See ed. R. Conquest, *Industrial Workers in the USSR*, Bodley Head, London, 1967, pp. 34–35; R. Hutchings, 'The ending of unemployment in the USSR', in *Soviet Studies*, July 1967.
8. See Nove, *The Soviet Economy*, 3rd ed., p. 135.
9. V. Gusev, 'Ishchem spetsialistov', in *Izvestiya*, 7 February 1973, p. 4.
10. See 'O dopolnenii Polozheniya o vysshikh i srednikh spetsial'-nykh uchebnykh zavedeniyakh SSSR', in *Byulleten' Ministerstva Vysshego Obrazovaniya*, 1/65, p. 11; ibid.
11. See, for example, V. Bocharov, 'Beglets', in *Komsomol'skaya Pravda*, 13 May 1967, p. 2.
12. As I observed while a student at the Tashkent Institute of National Economy.
13. See letter from Konovalova and report by G. Voshchin, in *Komsomol'skaya Pravda*, 16 January 1968, p. 1.
14. Statement by N. N. Panov, in *Komsomol'skaya Pravda*, 30 January 1968, p. 1.
15. I heard of this from more than one source while resident in the USSR. I have not seen any documentary confirmation.
16. See R. Conquest, *The Great Terror*, Macmillan, London, 1968, pp. 529–532.
17. For details on NKVD industrial activities, see S. Swianiewicz, *Forced Labour and Economic Development*, Oxford University Press, London, 1965, Appendix.
18. See ibid., pp. 14–15.
19. For a discussion of quotas for bookings among American traffic cops see J. Q. Wilson, *Varieties of Police Behaviour*, Harvard University Press Cambridge, Mass., 1968, pp. 53–54.
20. See D. J. Dallin and B. I. Nicolaevsky, *Forced Labour in Soviet Russia*, Hollis, London, 1948, pp. 212–213.
21. See Conquest, *op. cit.*, pp. 358–359.
22. Schwarz, *op. cit.*, p. 57.
23. See E. C. Brown, *Soviet Trade Unions and Labor Relations*, Harvard University Press, Cambridge, Mass., 1966, p. 31.

24. See leader in *Pravda*, 7 August 1974.
25. A 1971 report from Kazakhstan, relating to the development of Turgai *oblast*ı, indicates instructions to local *Komsomol* organizations on sources and types of specialists to be mobilized of such detail as to indicate strong pressurization as the only possible basis for implementation. See 'Turgai zovet', in *Kazakhstanskaya Pravda*, 12 January 1971, p. 3.
26. Nigel Grant, *Soviet Education*, 3rd ed., Penguin, Harmondsworth, 1972, p. 15.
27. 'A esli vniknutı', in *Pravda*, 15 November 1968, p. 2.
28. See Grant, *op. cit.*, especially Chapters 3, 4 and 5.
29. See A. P. Khodzhaev, 'Sostoyanie i zadachi nauchnoi organizatsii truda v promyshlennosti Uzbekistana', in *Ekonomika i Zhiznı*, 11 December 1969; I. Maslova, V. Moskovich, 'Puti uluchsheniya professionalno-kvalifikatsionnoi struktury kadrov i ikh ispolızovaniya v promyshlennosti', in *Voprosy Ekonomiki*, 3/70, p. 97; G. Snezhko, 'NOT i effektivnostı proizvodstva', in *Turkmenskaya Iskra*, 18 January 1973, p. 2.
30. See ed. Lupton, *op. cit.*, especially Part I.
31. See T. Wilson, *Inflation*, Blackwell, Oxford, 1961, Chapter 8.
32. A. Solomakhin, 'Ukrali voskresenıe', in *Pravda*, 14 January 1969, p. 2.
33. See P. Hanson, *The Consumer in the Soviet Economy*, Macmillan, London, 1968.
34. V. Shubkin, 'O konkretnykh issledovaniyakh sotsialınykh protsessov', in *Kommunist*, 3/65, p. 52.
35. V. Ignatenko, 'Severyanin', in *Komsomolıskaya Pravda*, 11 July 1967, p. 2.
36. See V. Andriyanov, 'Problemy kadrov dalınego vostoka; 2. pereselenets', in *Komsomolıskaya Pravda*, 24 July 1971, p. 2.
37. A. Gladyshev, 'Obshchestvennye fondy potreblenia i migratsiya naseleniya', in *Planovoe Khozyaistvo*, 10/66, pp. 18–19.
38. Published in *Pravda*, 27 September 1967.
39. See Gladyshev, *op. cit.*; Ya. Buzaev, 'Voprosy territorialınogo planirovaniya proizvodstva', in *Planovoe Khozyaistvo*, 12/68, pp. 34–39; J. A. Newth, 'The 1970 Soviet Census', in *Soviet Studies*, October 1972. The important exception to the

general trends is the fairly high rate of net immigration into the Baltic republics.

40. G. Dil'dyaev, 'Zakhochu i uplechu', in *Kazakhstanskaya Pravda*, 14 May 1972, p. 4.
41. V. Vasil'ev, *et al.*, 'Po sobstvennomu zhelaniyu', in *Molodoi Kommunist*, 1/66, pp. 34–35.
42. L. Alonov, 'Znakom'tes'': sluzhba trudoustroistva', in *Kommunist Tadzhikistana*, 20 January 1973, p. 3.
43. In the early stages of the construction of the Bratsk HES, for example, workers and their families were living in tents. See ed. V. F. Mal'tsev, *Bratskaya GES. Sbornik Dokumentov i Materialov*, Vol. I, pp. 72–76.
44. For an account of various studies done by Soviet sociologists on the subject of alienation among workers see G. Fischer, 'Sociology', in ed. G. Fischer, *Science and Ideology in Soviet Society*, Atherton Press, New York, 1967.
45. The precise date of their abolition is, however, uncertain. It is argued in ed. Conquest, *Industrial Workers ...*, (p. 23n.) that it must have been before 1933.
46. A. Larionov, 'Sluzhba truda', in *Komsomol'skaya Pravda*, 20 July 1971, p. 2.
47. Alonov, *op. cit.*; F. Zikrinov and A. Zuikov, 'Chemu uchit eksperiment', in *Kazakhstanskaya Pravda*, 14 September 1973, p. 2.
48. See *Radyans'ka Ukrayina*, 15 August 1973, p. 3, as abstracted in *ABSEES*, January 1974, p. 45.
49. Larionov, *op. cit.*
50. See 'Ne chislom, a umen'em', by P. Sharov, director of the Shchekino chemical *kombinat*, in *Pravda*, 30 November 1968, p. 2.
51. See 'Bol'she produktsii s men'shei chislennost'yu rabotnikov', in *Ekonomicheskaya Gazeta*, 10/70.
52. S. Shkurko, 'Voprosy stimulirovaniya proizvoditel'nosti truda', in *Planovoe Khozyaistvo*, 7/71, p. 10.
53. See P. J. D. Wiles, 'A note on Soviet unemployment on US definitions', in *Soviet Studies*, April 1972.
54. See Brown, *op. cit.*, p. 70.
55. See, for example, I. Novikov, 'Edut na zavod delegatsii', in *Pravda*, 9 May 1974, p. 2, in which the message seems to be: combine socialist competition with NOT.

56. See Schwarz, *op. cit.*, pp. 193–199.
57. Brown, *op. cit.*, pp. 56–57.
57. Ibid., p. 181.
59. See, for example, V. Zhukov, 'Sovershenstvuyem kachestvo rassmotreniya grazhdanskikh del', in *Sovetskaya Yustitsiya*, 15/65, pp. 9–10; letter from G. Treilib, in *Pravda*, 19 January 1967, p. 2; V. Gorodetskii, 'S pozitsii nablyudatelei', in *Trud*, 1 December 1967, p. 2; report of speech by D. Karaev at the XX Congress of the CP of Turkmenistan, in *Turkmenskaya Iskra*, 23 February 1971, p. 2.
60. V. Konyshev, 'Mozhno li s etim mirit'sya?', in *Izvestiya*, 6 February 1973, p. 2.
61. See M. Bazarbaeva, 'Kakoi detsad v vashem kolkhoze?' in *Kommunist Tadzhikistana*, 1 September 1972, p. 2; leader in *Sovetskaya Moldaviya*, 13 October 1972, p. 1.
62. A. E. Probst, *Voprosy Razmeshcheniya Sotsialisticheskoi Promyshlennosti*, Nauka, Moscow, 1971, pp. 163–164.
63. The lady in question is Ye. A. Furtseva. See Fainsod, *op. cit.*
64. For a detailed discussion of the whole issue of female employment see N. T. Dodge, *Women in the Soviet Economy*, Oxford University Press, London, 1967.
65. See Brown, *op. cit.*, pp. 234–235.

CHAPTER SEVEN

The Agricultural Sector

It is always particularly necessary to bear in mind long-run historical 'regularities' and socio-political variables when dealing with non-urban production activity. In the case of Soviet agriculture, however, where the decision to go for mass collectivization was inextricably bound up with the whole strategy of industrial development, and where the rate of change of the economic and extra-economic variables affecting agriculture has been enormously swift, we witness an extraordinary concretization and intensification of this basic generalization. We must recognize that the experience of the agricultural sector in the Soviet Union has been, in a very real sense, unique.

There is no need in the present context to describe in detail the forced transition from individual peasant to large-scale collectivized agriculture.[1] It is, however, worth stressing that opposition to collectivization on the part of the mass of the middle peasantry as well as the rich peasants should not necessarily be taken as an indication of any antipathy, traditional or otherwise, towards collective or co-operative modes of life and work. True, pre-First World War developments had been away from the traditional communalism of the *mir* towards a more individualistic type of farming. But since the policies of prime minister Peter Stolypin were expressly aimed at just this end, we cannot assume that the trend represented any significant change in peasant psychology. The system which the peasantry, with very little interference from Bolsheviks or indeed anyone else from the towns, established in the wake of the revolution of February 1917 was equalitarian in terms of land distribution and fairly traditional in terms of the role allocated to the village assembly.[2] A process of economic differentiation certainly set in during the 1920s, but there is little evidence to suggest that it had by 1928 proceeded far enough to destroy the basic sense of solidarity and community in the village. What the peasantry opposed was a system of collectivization emanating from outside and enforced in the crudest way. Any discussion of the problems of Soviet agriculture, and how they might be overcome, must be carried on with this firmly in mind.

As we noted in Chapter One, the decision to collectivize was anything but the culmination of a carefully thought-out strategy. One of the key elements in the situation was the existence of a serious short-term procurements problem. During the winter of 1927/28, long before the industrialization drive got seriously under way, it became clear that there was going to be a serious shortfall in grain procurements. How were the towns to be fed? Stalin's answer was the 'Urals-Siberian method', i.e. a return to the practice of *prodraztverstka* – compulsory procurement – *à la* War Communism. Once some element of coercion has been reintroduced, it may be argued, the transition to a greater degree of coercion is hardly surprising. But a more systematic interpretation can be placed on the escalation of coercion. The winter of 1927/28 ended the town–country *smychka* (alliance) of NEP irrevocably. Had Stalin wanted another NEP it would have taken him a decade to build it up. Once the confidence of the peasantry that the 'rules of the game' would be observed had been shattered, the vicious circle of reductions in sowings, concealment of production, deepening of the procurements crisis and increased severity of procurements measures was surely inevitable. It is significant that centralized procurements in 1928/29 were actually below the level of 1927/28.[3] It became clear that efficient procurement by coercive means demanded the establishment of control over production itself. As the industrialization drive gathered momentum, and issues of savings and investment rates began to overshadow issues of commodity flows *per se*, collectivization presented itself as a way of killing two birds with one stone, of solving the short-term problem of maintaining the supply of food to the towns, and the long-term problem of ensuring a source of finance for the grandiose tasks of the five-year plans.

Why was collectivization implemented in such a crude way? Even if we accept that it had to be a military campaign, we do not have to accept that it had to be such a badly run one. But organizational factors may not have been the only important ones here. The Bolsheviks were, by ideology and inclination, unsympathetic to and highly suspicious of the peasantry.[4] One remembers Gor'kii's dictum that Soviet Russia's best hope was that 'the half-savage, stupid and dull people of the Russian villages and countryside will die out'.[5]

We are left, however, trying to explain the fact that so little guidance on precisely how collectivization should be implemented was forthcoming from the leadership. A contemporary Soviet historian's work on Azerbaidzhan, for example, shows how the campaign in that republic was characterized by vagueness and confusion on basic matters of policy.[6] Stalin's 1930 article 'Dizzy with success',[7] which accused local cadres of errors and excesses, came like a bolt from the blue, and the resultant temporary retreat was soon followed by a new campaign as violent and hurried as the first. The paradox of this anarchic birth of the centrally planned Soviet system may be explicable, as Alec Nove has suggested, quite simply in terms of Stalin's refusal to compromise in any way with the myth of the spontaneous origin of the collectivization movement.[9] In any case, the chaos of the campaign had immediate and drastic effects on the agricultural sector. The recalcitrant peasants proceeded to slaughter more than 50 per cent of the total livestock, while cadres concentrated on organizational questions. In 1933 there supervened a famine of terrible proportions, which resulted in the deaths, through starvation, of millions, and hit the Ukraine particularly badly.[10] But procurements were soon established at a high level, while supplies from the industrial sector remained minimal. No doubt the authorities would, if possible, have lived up to the slogans about deliveries of machinery, etc., to the new collectives, but the ambitiousness of industrial plans left this, in practice, out of the question. Procurement prices were set at such a low level – in fact sometimes not even covering transport costs[11] – that ideological compromise was necessary in order to ensure the physical survival of the peasants. Each peasant was permitted to hold a small piece of land – the 'private plot', adequate for vegetable-growing, chicken-raising, and the grazing of a cow or goat. The role of these plots was not, however, to be a purely subsistence one. They were to provide a considerable percentage of the supply of many agricultural products to the urban sector. Up till comparatively recently, in fact, the vast bulk of the egg supply to Soviet towns came from the 'private subsidiary sector'.[12] It is, then, perhaps not surprising that the sector was subjected to heavy rates of taxation.[13]

Between 1928 and 1953 Soviet agricultural output virtually stagnated, as Table 6 indicates.

TABLE 6
Soviet Agricultural Output 1928–53
(1913 equals 100)

1928	124	1945	86
1933	101	1947	122
1937	134	1950	140
1939	121	1951	130
1940	141	1953	146

SOURCE
Narodnoe Khozyaistvo SSSR v 1961 godu, Gosstatizdat, Moscow, 1961, p. 292.

Karcz has shown, however, that performance over this period in terms of foodstuff procurements, production of industrial crops, and even exports of agricultural products, is very much more impressive.[14] In addition, labour was released to man the fast developing industrial sector (see Chapter Six), while the high level of procurements, coupled with the low level of procurement prices, ensured that the peasantry contributed a large share to the savings/investment effort necessary to support industrial development plans. A certain degree of caution must, however, be exercised on this last point, perhaps the most fundamental of all. Living standards were very depressed amongst almost all sections of the Soviet population in the early and middle 1930s,[15] and it has been suggested that the contribution of the agricultural sector in the crucial formative prewar period may have been relatively less important than it was in the immediate postwar period.[16]

Whatever standpoint one may take on particular aspects, the fact emerges quite starkly that the whole development (if one can call it such) of Soviet agriculture during the Stalin period was essentially negative with respect to the agricultural sector itself.

But by the early 1950s the policy of going for procurements rather than production, starving the sector of investment, and providing no real incentive to increase production, or indeed to do anything in the collective sector, was moving towards its inevitable come-uppance. It is possible for only so long to continue taking a larger share from a more or less constant total. The problem that Stalin left for his successors was not so very different from that of 1927/28 – how to feed the towns.

It is most important to bear in mind that the damage that has been done to Soviet agriculture in the quarter century of the Stalin period went further than the imposition of an alien form of collective, a low standard of living and a low rate of investment. Vast sociological changes had taken place which cannot be blamed on shortcomings in government tactics, or even on the fact of using compulsion itself. So many of the things that happened during the period drained the lifeblood out of agriculture, by depriving it, quite literally, of its manhood. The men who left for the towns and factories in the 1930s, who left for the front in 1942 – and in many cases never came back, or if they did, often had no inclination to return to their native village – were the men of young to middle age who must form the basis of a strong labour force, particularly in a business requiring physique and stamina as well as skill and experience. Certainly the 'dekulakization' aspect of collectivization contributed to this tendency. Certainly the war losses which the Soviet Union suffered can only be described as extraordinary.[17] But the general point remains that any country which embarks on a policy of rapid industrialization, starting off from a position of predominantly peasant economy, is bound to face this kind of problem.

Before going on to discuss the agricultural policies of Stalin's successors, we must pause to add some flesh to the skeleton outline of the system of agricultural administration given in Chapter One. The system imposed in the early 1930s did, in fact, survive in its main elements until the middle 1960s. In addition to market, or quasi-market, instruments of taxation and supplies and equipment prices, *kolkhozy* were subjected to command elements through fixed procurement prices and obligatory minimum deliveries to the state procurement organs. Produce beyond these minimum quotas could be sold to the state authorities, usually at a higher price, or alternatively sold on the *kolkhoz* market – the institution principally orientated to the sale of produce from peasants' private plots – at free market prices. Needless to say, pressures to sell surplus to the state rather than on the free market were not infrequently felt.

Even this, however, gives little of the true flavour of the reality of the collective farm under Stalin. Chairmen were in practice imposed from above, and were often not local men, or even countrymen.[18] In addition, *kolkhozy* were subject to systematic (or perhaps we should say unsystematic!) interference from outside, particularly from the Communist Party. Local Party cadres in rural areas were seen as bearing a responsibility for 'their' farms which went beyond mere supervision. Then there were Party 'plenipoten-tiaries' (*upolnomochennye*), always quite likely to descend on a farm, organizing campaigns, setting 'additional' targets and so on, often on the basis of little knowledge of local conditions and problems.

It is significant, if ironic, that the one aspect of the formal col-lectivist structure that really meant what it said was the principle whereby payment was in the form of a share of the residual after obligations had been met, rather than of a wage payment. The precise level of the share was determined on the basis of the number of *trudodni* (singular *trudoden*¹), or conventional work days, a *kolkhoznik* had to his credit. In practice, the residual left at the end of the year tended often to be so small that the system, far from operating as a profit-sharing scheme, functioned simply as a device for pushing down peasant incomes from the collective sector to a minimum, and of forcing the peasantry to bear the risks of bad harvests and other natural calamities. The procure-ment price system, with its low compulsory quota prices but higher additional delivery prices, meant that low aggregate production levels hit the peasants particularly hard. It is not sur-prising, in view of all this, that the average *kolkhoznik* concentrated as much as possible on his own little plot, and did as little as he could get away with on the *kolkhoz* – hence, of course, the intro-duction, in 1939, of legislation establishing that *kolkhozniki* were obliged to work a certain minimum number of days per year on the collective farm.[19]

Though formally identical with state industrial enterprises, state farms (*sovkhozy*) operated under a peculiarly liberal financial regime. Many *sovkhozy* received considerable subsidies from the central authorities, quite apart from the preferential treatment they received, compared with *kolkhozy*, in terms of taxation and equipment prices (investment for *sovkhozy*, as for other state enterprises, proceeded on the basis of grants to 1965). State farm workers received fixed basic wage payments, and were, understandably usually much better off than collective farm workers. The *sovkhozy*, however, were just as subject to the arbitrary attentions of the cadres as were the *kolkhozy*, and indeed were the chosen instruments of the Virgin Lands scheme, perhaps the greatest political initiative of all.[20]

Khrushchev was interested in agriculture, in a way that Stalin never was, and in a way that was not characteristically Bolshevik. During Stalin's last years Khrushchev was very much involved in major agricultural policies. The process of amalgamation and enlargement of *kolkhozy* which began around 1950, and which carried on throughout the 1950s, seems to have originated with the initiative of Nikita Sergeevich. Connected with this was the idea of 'agro-towns', large, quasi-urban settlements in the countryside, rejected at the time, however, and never seriously reintroduced by Khrushchev.[21] What is noteworthy is that the whole amalgamation policy seems basically to have had a political motive – namely that with a shortage of party cadres and reliable chairmen in the countryside, the interests of control are best served by using big units, so that the scarce resource can be efficiently spread. The interest in agro-towns showed a preparedness to think in terms of pumping resources into agriculture, but apart from this there was little enough indication of what was to come.

In the 'collective leadership' which succeeded Stalin it was Khrushchev, holding the position of First Secretary of the Communist Party, who took primary responsibility for agriculture, and who soon announced plans for radical departures in policy on the sector. General measures included improved procurement prices, relaxation of taxation on private plots, and a programme for increased production of agricultural machinery and fertilizers. This last was, of course, a necessary condition for any increase in investment and the raising of the technological level of agriculture, short of massive imports. But Khrushchev's plans did not stop at general measures, important as these were. A great new Virgin Lands scheme was announced.

In the southern part of the Soviet heartland – South-East

European Russia, South-West Siberia and North Kazakhstan – the land is fairly arid steppe, and had never been systematically cultivated. Now, however, a campaign was to be mounted aimed at bringing vast tracts of land in this area under continuous cultivation, with the construction and development of giant state farms. The aim was primarily to increase grain production, but it was also hoped that livestock production would benefit indirectly, with the traditional grain-growing areas of the Ukraine being able to shift greater emphasis on to fodder crops.[22] An intense political campaign was mounted to aid in the manning of the project (see Chapter Six).

Khrushchev's agricultural policies showed immediate success. By 1958 gross agricultural output, according to official figures, was standing at 49 per cent above the 1953 figure, with a corresponding figure for grain production alone of 71 per cent.[23] Agriculture seemed to have broken out of the vicious circle of a quarter of a century's stagnation. In 1958 a further major reform was announced. The machine-tractor stations (MTSs) were abolished. These stations had been organizations which rented out mechanized services of one kind or another to groups of collective farms. In principle, the idea had been that economies of scale should be exploited with operations like ploughing and sowing. In practice the role of the MTSs was much more of a political one – ensuring control by the central authorities in a sector where generalized hostility was the rule, and loyal cadres few and far between. In strictly economic terms their effect was often pernicious since their success-indicator regime was in terms of targets for sown area, ploughed area, etc. Inevitable clashes arose between MTSs and farms, even to the extent of the former ploughing up land unsolicited, just so as to have fulfilled the plan.[24] The amalgamation of collective farms had solved, at least partially, the political control problem, and had certainly increased scope for the exploitation of economies of scale within the boundaries of a single farm. Thus political and economic preconditions had been established for the transition to a rationalized system of agricultural management. A network of repair-technical stations (RTSs) was set up to provide for the maintenance of the equipment now transferred to the *kolkhozy*.

Another change which came in 1958 was the abolition of the multiple procurement price system. While in no sense representing a fundamental reform of prices, it did remove a feature which had always made things particularly difficult for poorer *kolkhozy*, and for all *kolkhozy* in years of bad harvest. The new system of 'sliding prices' aimed to push all prices up in bad harvest years, and down in good, though it is not clear that this ever really worked in practice.

The considerable successes of the 1953–58 period were not kept up in the years to follow. Gross agricultural production, which had grown so steadily during that period, stagnated over the following five years, and in 1963 actually stood at a slightly lower level than it had in 1958.[25] In 1963 it was, in fact, necessary to import massive quantities of grain from North America.[26] Now the exceptionally poor performance of agriculture in 1963 can be attributed partly to bad weather, but quite clearly something had gone wrong with Khrushchev's agricultural policies.

At the most general level the successes of the earlier period had been on the basis of extensive rather than intensive development. Yields had risen much less than output, and you cannot go on increasing cultivated area indefinitely. To explain the severity of the setback, however, we must refer to a number of more specific factors.

The Virgin Lands scheme, initially so successful, started to run into trouble in the late 1950s and early 1960s, as the figures in Table 7 show.

TABLE 7

Gross output of grain products (in 000 of tons)

	1950	1954–58 av.	1958	1959	1960	1962	1963
Western Siberia	7,270	12,817	14,491	12,502	14,458	9,054	4,987
Kazakh-stan	4,747	13,760	21,952	19,085	18,693	15,888	10,592

NOTE

The Virgin Lands area is not, of course, identical with Western Siberia and Kazakhstan, and the figures given can only be taken as a rough indication of developments in the areas newly brought under cultivation.

SOURCES

Various editions of *Narodnoe Khozyaistvo SSSR*.

Occasional very bad harvests were only of course, to be expected in such an arid region, but there is a systematic downward trend after 1958. The essence of the problem was really quite simple. The whole scheme was aimed basically at increasing aggregate output, particularly of wheat, and increasing it fast. Khrushchev wanted continuous cultivation of the area, and the nature of the command system ensured that this, to a great extent, was what happened. But with marginal lands, short of rainfall, it is necessary to take particular care to prevent the emergence of dustbowl phenomena. In order to ensure that the precious topsoil is not blown away under such conditions it is not sufficient just to practise crop rotation. The land really has to be left fallow from time to time.[27] But the perfectly understandable obsession with raising output as much as possible, coupled with Khrushchev's general anti-grassland attitude,[28] meant that this need was often ignored. As a result, severe erosion symptoms began to appear in the late 1950s,[29] and this must have been the major factor in the tendency to sharp decline in harvest levels.

Whatever the basic soundness of the decision to abolish the MTSs, certain aspects of the policy are open to criticism. The collective farms had to pay for the equipment transferred to their ownership, and this, combined with Khrushchev's insistence that the price improvements of the 1950s had been sufficient and would not be repeated, meant a heavy financial burden for many collectives, a drop in living standards for *kolkhozniki*,[30] and of course reduced capacity to undertake new investment. The 1959 peak level of 3,526,000 roubles of fixed investment by *kolkhozy* was not surpassed until 1964.[31] Thus incentives were weakened and technological re-equipment slowed down at a crucial time. In addition, the repair-technical stations did not operate well, and were in fact abolished in 1961, their functions being transferred to a new body concerned with the supply of equipment, etc., to farms called *sel'khoztekhnika*. As Erich Strauss has said, however:

> This was less a solution of a difficult problem than a shrugging-off of its existence, and the result was a serious fall in the already low level of maintenance and repairs of agricultural plant.[32]

But the abolition of the MTSs never meant any reduction in the general exposure of the farm sector to political pressure of one kind or another. It merely meant that the local Party men were left with a clear field. About this time, for example, Khrushchev began to make pronouncements whose gist was that the peasants were spending too much time on their private plots. As a result, the years that followed were characterized by various forms of pressure being put on peasants by local Party cadres which significantly reduced the head of livestock held in the private sector, and also the actual area of land held in the sector.[33]

Khrushchev was a man for 'brainwaves', or, as his denouncers put it later on, 'hare-brained schemes'. Perhaps the best known of these, apart from the Virgin Lands, which comes into a rather special category, is the Maize Campaign. Noting that animal products of all kinds continued to be in great shortage, and noting that in order to produce animal products you first of all need fodder, Nikita Sergeevich developed a great enthusiasm for maize. This enthusiasm gained the status of official policy as early as 1955,[34] though the Maize Campaign proper did not get into full swing until the late 1950s and early 1960s. Now the point about maize in the Soviet Union is that many areas are unsuitable for its cultivation. The campaign, however, tended to ignore regional variations, and there were indeed attempts to grow maize in the north-western economic region – in the same latitudes as Scandinavia.[35] How far this inflexibility was the personal responsibility of Khrushchev, and how far 'a function of the system', raises general issues to which we shall return later. What is beyond doubt is that large areas of land were switched from an optimal to a sub-optimal, sometimes grossly sub-optimal, crop-pattern, and that the Maize Campaign deprived the grain sector of land while failing to make spectacular contributions in the livestock sector.[36]

An interesting development which coincided with the peak of the Maize Campaign, and which may have partially reflected a desire on the part of Khrushchev to modify the inflexibility of the implementation of the campaign, came in 1961, with the formation of the so-called territorial-production administrations (*territorial¹ no-proizvodstvennye upravleniya*), local agricultural management bodies covering areas intermediate in size between *oblast¹* and *raion*. Undoubtedly one of the factors contributing to the problems of agriculture in the late Khrushchev period was the leader's penchant for continual administrative reshuffling – we have already seen this kind of thing in the industrial sphere. But the 1962 change, while ineffectual enough in itself, illustrates very graphically the kind of problems Khrushchev was up against. As he said when introducing the reform:

> We have abandoned the old system of planning, have condemned the bad practice of handing down plans for sown areas from above, and were right in doing so. But some comrades, as is now evident, have an over-simplified concept of the new system of planning, and consider rejection of the planning of sown areas from above as rejection of any intervention in the planning of collective and state farm production.
> This is incorrect. We abandoned an approach to planning which erroneously tried to fix the plan for sowing of individual crops on each collective and state farm from above, because it is impossible for the centre to take account of the specific features of each zone. But the planning of production and procurements on the collective and state farms must be a firm rule and law. Naturally, therefore, once the plan is drawn up and the assignment given, the production administration, in order to know how the collective farms are coping with fulfilment of their pledges, should conduct check-ups, and rapidly eliminate any shortcomings that come to light.[37]

This passage gives us a clue to at least one of the basic reasons why Khrushchev's agricultural policies, after such a bright start, eventually disappointed. It has often been remarked that the First Secretary, for all his penchant for change, was unable to conceive of radical reform in approach. His whole training and experience had been in terms of 'hurrah' planning (his big early success was as trouble-shooter on the building of the Moscow Metro)[38] and he could not conceive of an agricultural policy except in terms of something imposed from above. Just precisely how 'above' was something that Khrushchev thought about a great deal but his 'decentralization' in agriculture, like his 'decentralization' in industry, turned out to be essentially simply a regionalization or localization of the traditional administrative approach.

Should all the blame be laid, then, at the personal door of Nikita Sergeevich? Surely not. We must bear in mind that the sort of human raw material available on the collective farms was, for the various historical reasons discussed earlier, not exactly highly suitable for the assumption of new responsibilities. It is quite wrong to assume that just because the peasants did not like the collectives as they were, they would throw themselves with enthusiasm into some new system which allowed them much more initiative – especially since many of them were really much too old to throw themselves, with the best will in the world, very far at all. If major changes in crop patterns, major changes in agricultural technology, etc., were what was required, and required quickly, then the initiative would have to come from somewhere in the government/party hierarchy – all the more so with a pioneering project like the Virgin Lands. But you cannot have a system based on instructions and campaigns – i.e. the principles of command and priority – without getting distortions. We have already seen the sort of thing that happens in industry, and there can be no reason to believe that an agricultural hierarchy will operate in any way differently from an industrial hierarchy. The problem which the command system finds most difficult to cope with, indeed the very rock on which it founders, is the problem of heterogeneity. Now there is nothing as heterogeneous as agriculture, particularly in a country which covers one-sixth of the globe, and where climatic conditions vary from frozen wasteland to desert.

We are now getting to the real kernel of the problem that faced Khrushchev in the agricultural sector. The difficulties that agriculture faced in the 1950s were essentially long-term difficulties partly connected with the decisions taken around 1930. In addition, just as in 1927–30. There were short-term problems of great and increasing urgency. In fact, the immediate problem of the early 1950s was identical to that of the late 1920s, namely not enough grain to feed the towns, irrespective of any question of investment, or industrialization, or growth plans, or anything else. The difference was that in the early 1950s the policy of going for procurements rather than production had come to the arithmetically inevitable end of the trail, and Khrushchev had to go for an increase in actual production, and quickly. It was not primarily a matter of redressing a sectoral imbalance, of revitalizing a depressed sector (cf. UK regional policy), or even of removing a constraint that would eventually or even immediately seriously affect overall growth rates. It was quite simply and starkly that there was not enough food to go round, and on top of this the post-Stalin leadership wanted to raise living standards!

It is quite clear that Khrushchev failed to solve finally any of the long-term problems of agriculture. It is not so clear that he failed in terms of the immediate short run – after all production did increase by 50 per cent in the period 1953–58, and the USSR managed to continue to feed itself, however badly. The trouble was that by 1963 the situation was once more one of immediate crisis – hence the imports from North America – because the underlying continuing crisis had not been solved.

But it would be totally unfair to say that Khrushchev ignored the need for long-term solutions. Improvements in agricultural prices and, as a corollary, increases in peasant incomes and investment flows into agriculture, would obviously form the cornerstone of any long-term strategy, and these very policies were, of course, pioneered by Khrushchev. The point is that the First Secretary's overriding concern with short-term results led him to seek panaceas which, even if perfectly reasonable in principle, tended to be implemented in such a way as to create rather than solve problems in the long run. The manner of implementation of these panaceas is something that we can, perhaps, lay at the door of the system. The decision to go for 'schemes' in the first place, at the cost of tying up resources which could have been devoted to strengthening the basic investment/peasant incomes push, was Khrushchev's. In addition, the totally negative attitude to any form or degree of devolution of genuine decision-making power to the peasants was encouraged, if not originated, by Khrushchev. The policy of restricting the private sector may, indeed, have been as much a reflection of this as of sheer ideological prejudice. Decentralization would not have helped much in the short run, and indeed would have been totally out of context, and probably counter-productive, in the big campaigns. But some movement, even if partial and selective, in the direction of autonomy for the rural producing unit was surely an essential precondition of the success of the genuinely far-sighted elements in Khrushchev's policies.

This, then, was the Khrushchevian dilemma. It is both significant and ironic that one of the First Secretary's last major departures in agricultural policy – the splitting of the Party itself into separate hierarchies for industry and agriculture – was as ineffectual as an administrative reform as it was unpopular among the cadres. It may have been nothing more than bureaucratic musical chairs, but the Party had had enough, and this was clearly a factor in Khrushchev's removal in 1964.[39]

We have been a long time in arriving at the agricultural policies of the post-Khrushchev leadership, but it is only against the background of the cruel dilemmas going back to 1927 that we can fully understand these policies. In one sense, Brezhnev/Kosygin/ Podgorny simply cut the Gordian knot, inasmuch as they relaxed the requirement that the Soviet Union should normally be self-sufficient in foodstuffs. The relaxation was marginal – there is no question of the Soviet Union ceasing, as a matter of policy, to be predominantly self-sufficient. But by accepting North American grain deliveries as more or less normal, the new leadership gave themselves a breathing space which Khrushchev had never really had.[40]

Immediately on taking power the new leadership abolished the TPAs and replaced them with a more conventional system based on the Ministry of Agriculture. The division of the Party into two hierarchies was reversed. Then at the March 1965 Plenum of the CC/CPSU a package of new measures for agriculture was announced. The main thrust of the package was a re-emphasis on the policy of improving peasant incomes and investment flows into agriculture, by raising prices, reducing taxation, and increasing the production of agricultural equipment and fertilizers. This had, of course, been an original plank of the Khrushchev platform, but had been effectively in abeyance since 1958. In addition, the restrictions on private plots which had been a feature of post-1958 policies were relaxed.[41] One rather odd feature of the new policy was a return to the two-tiered procurement price system for grain.

As we have seen, one of the major elements in the 'continuous demoralization' of the peasantry was the *trudoden*[1] system. A few collective farms had already gone over to a system of guaranteed minimum monthly wage payments before the advent of the new leadership,[42] but it was in mid-1966 that the system was introduced as a general measure.[43] By 1969 about 95 per cent of *kolkhozy* were on guaranteed monthly payments.[44] This development reflected a change in approach which had already been hinted at in the early measures of the new leadership, in particular by the fiscal reform which abolished the time-honoured practice of counting payments to peasants as part of *kolkhoz* income for taxation purposes.[45] The reader should note the connection between this aspect of policy and trends in the overall financial position of collective farms. A *kolkhoz* has to be fairly strong to be able to afford to pay regular monthly salaries, and, looking at it from the other direction, a regular monthly salary is only meaningful if it is at a reasonably high level. According to one calculation, average *kolkhoznik* income from the collective farm climbed from 325 roubles per annum in 1960 to 763 roubles per annum in 1967 – the latter figure comparing with around 1,000 roubles per annum for *sovkhoz* workers.[46] An estimate for 1969–70 rates average *kolkhoznik* income as 87 per cent of the corresponding figure for *sovkhoz* workers.[47] In 1975 average *kolkhoznik* income seems to have stabilized at about 70–75 per cent of average urban worker income. None of these figures, of course, take account of earnings from the sale of private plot produce. The 1970 decree extending state social insurance benefits to *kolkhozniki* continued the trend to improvement in the material lot of the peasantry.

The other main thrust of post-Khrushchev policy has been in the direction of regularizing the relationship between the central authorities and the farm, and here we find a complete break with the Khrushchev tradition. Not only was there a strong movement away from 'voluntarism', but a cautious movement towards genuine decentralization could even be detected.

'The very word plenipotentiary has been abolished,' declared L. Yagodin in 1968.[48] While there was to be no renunciation of the special responsibility of the Party for agriculture, policy was set quite firmly against the kind of arbitrary *deus/diabolus ex machina* approach which had been equally common under Stalin and Khrushchev. The Party would now be restricted to an 'advisory' role. Now students of Communist systems have heard this one before, but there can at least be no doubt of the strength and sincerity of the original intention.

A measure which can perhaps be seen as a part of the same overall policy thrust is the *sovkhoz* planning reform of 1967. Basically what this measure meant was that *sovkhozy* would now be on full *khozraschet*, i.e. they would no longer automatically have losses covered by the budget, but would operate on the same set of indicators as reformed industrial enterprises, i.e. principally sales and profit, and would undertake investment on the basis of retained profits or loans, rather than grants. In addition to the rather marginal degree of decentralization which the reform in general granted, *sovkhoz* directors were given special rights to dismiss labour if they deemed it necessary, and to sell freely stocks of perishable goods refused by procurement agencies. This, then, seems to have represented a genuine move towards greater autonomy for the producer unit, as well as regularizing the position of the *sovkhoz*.[49]

Perhaps the most interesting of the post-Khrushchev developments has been the renewed interest shown in the so-called 'link' (*zveno*, plural *zven'ya*) system. The principal form of organization within the *kolkhoz* and *sovkhoz* has, throughout the history of post-collectivization agriculture, been the brigade, A traditional brigade is a largish unit, up to 100 strong, performing general agricultural tasks. The link, in contrast, is a small unit, often of less than ten people, which is allocated a particular piece of land to work, or a particular specialized function. The link system had been favoured by Andreev, the agriculture boss in the late Stalin period, but was officially relegated to disfavour, along with Andreev himself, in 1950.[50] Interest in the link increased again in the late 1950s and early 1960s, and Khrushchev mounted another of his campaigns in its favour. The campaign was not particularly successful, and by 1962 the traditional predominance of the brigade was firmly re-established.[51] Experimental work on the link system did however continue, and under the new leadership interest in the alternative approach has again increased. The most interesting thing of all is that, in line with the policy of 'non-interference', the authorities have merely declared that *kolkhoz* and *sovkhoz* managements may go ahead with experiments along *zveno* lines if, and when, they wish. There has been no campaign.

The autonomous or 'normless' (*beznaryadnoe*) link, the type that has received most attention, is simply given a small piece of land, the necessary equipment, and told to get on with it. No set tasks as such are handed down, only a sales plan, and members share in the profits of overplan sales.[52] There has of course been a great deal of variation – understandably, given the policy of the authorities. But the primary emphasis has been on a 'land-attached' type of link, and this has reflected a recognition of the tremendous psychological importance of giving, or rather returning, to the peasants some real sense of 'mastery' of the land.[53] It is interesting that one of the reasons why the Khrushchev campaign was not altogether successful was that it was in this case the 'crop-attached' variant that was being pushed. The point is of course that the realities of crop rotation ensure that a unit specializing in a particular crop will by definition not be attached to a particular piece of land, so that one of the most important potential advantages of the system was lost.[54]

Success with the link has not been unqualified. One thing that has become clear is that it is no use establishing autonomous links if they cannot be adequately equipped.[55] Partly because of this, perhaps, the whole issue has, in a sense, been widened to encompass a general reappraisal of the internal organization of the *kolkhoz* and *sovkhoz*. Some farms, finding the link too small a unit, have stuck to the brigade, but have given it the same kind of autonomy as is associated with the link.[56] Others have developed the link as an autonomously organized purveyor of specialized services.[57] In the case of some *sovkhozy* major sub-divisions have been given fully independent status as specialized *sovkhozy*, and one source suggests that links should have the same status.[58] This, by the way, indicates that the title 'link' may apply to units much larger than the traditional *zveno*, and that we should, perhaps, not attach too much importance to titles.

It is clear that there are really two quite separate issues involved in the whole *zveno* discussion. The first one is the matter of giving a greater sense of involvement and job satisfaction to the peasants by allowing them to work in small groups, and to stick to one piece of land, which they can 'nurse'. It is significant that one of the things about the land-attached link that seems to worry conservatives is the fact that they often tend to be family units.[59] The second issue is that of the creation of integrated, well-equipped, autonomous sub-units on the farm, irrespective of size or function. The full importance of the distinction becomes clear when we consider one of the salient features of Soviet agriculture – the coexistence of overpopulation and underemployment in general with shortage of trained, skilled operatives, particularly in the mechanized field, a shortage intractable in the short run because so much tied up with the peculiar age and sex structure in the countryside.[60] It is perfectly obvious that the second aspect of trends in farm organization must run up against constraints of a demographic and sociological nature. It is less clear that the first should necessarily encounter the same problems. The small *zveno* must surely be a basically labour-intensive institution, and if family-based must surely be peculiarly well suited to getting the best out of the *babushki*. This is not to say that the Soviet authorities see the *zveno* in this way. But they are conscious of the problem of underemployment, as is evinced by their great interest in the development of industrial activities in the countryside.

The Russian climate makes underemployment problems during a long winter inevitable, whatever the general position, so that the concept of the agro-industrial combine has understandably had a special attraction for Soviet farms. The value of output from subsidiary industrial plants on *kolkhozy* and *sovkhozy* grew from 4,700 million roubles in 1966 to 6,600 million roubles in 1968,[61] after the publication, in 1967, of a new decree on the development of subsidiary enterprise. According to one estimate the figure would reach 15,000 million roubles by 1975.[62] Development of subsidiary enterprise has, however, been inhibited by a number of factors. Firstly, the authorities, both local and central, have shown some concern about the broader implications of building up an industrial sector essentially outside the control of the industrial planning apparatus.[63] In extreme cases agro-industrial combination has even been pictured as a hot-bed of quasi-private enterprise and speculation.[64] It is perhaps for this reason that the authorities have been keen to encourage the development of inter-*kolkhoz ob''edineniya*, and of mixed state-*kolkhoz ob''edineniya*, which appear to involve a much higher degree of central control.[65] Secondly, and related to the first point, there has been the problem of supplies for the agro-industrial sector. As we saw in Chapter Four in connection with decentralized investment, the post-1965 system has not been able effectively to integrate partial decentralization into the general environment of central planning, and the agro-industrial sector has suffered from this as well.[66] Lastly, and in some senses most fundamentally, the kind of labour which predominates in abundance in the countryside – elderly people, largely female, may not be amenable to transfer on to even relatively simple factory work.[67] It is significant that one estimate puts the proportion of *kolkhozniki* working in inter-*kolkhoz ob''edineniya* in the Ukraine around 1970 as only one-third of the total workforce.[68] For all these drawbacks, however, the concept of the agro-industrial combine must figure strongly in any long-term development strategy for agriculture, particularly since it permits the transfer of labour from agriculture without involving society in the cost of shifting them from a rural to an urban milieu – cf. the discussion of urban external diseconomies in Chapter Five. Any ideological inhibitions must surely be quickly removed by reference to Engels' discussion of the removal of the distinction between town and country under Full Communism.[69]

The prospects for Soviet agriculture at the present moment are uncertain. Gross agricultural production has grown by 43 per cent over the period 1965–73.[70] On the other hand, the poor harvests of 1972 and 1975 were setbacks and emphasized the extent to which the harvest is still subject to Mother Nature's whirls. Agricultural productivity, in any case, remains very low, and there can be no question of the problem of food supply in the Soviet Union having been finally solved. Subordination of long-term to short-term needs has always been the curse of Soviet agricultural policies, admittedly often under very great pressure. The pressure has slackened somewhat, if only because of a greater willingness to participate in international exchange. But the recent instability of US policy on grain exports must have shown the Soviet leadership just how many hostages to fortune may be involved in international exchange, even in conditions of *détente*.[71] The real danger of course is that renewed feelings of pressure may result in a return to more traditional ways of coping with crisis. It is perfectly clear that the old habits of *apparatchik* arbitrariness have been dying hard,[72] and the replacement of Matskevich, the veteran Minister for Agriculture, by the Party apparatus man Polyanskii in 1973 may have done little to keep policy on its original course. The 1974 publicity on the need for reconstruction in the non-black earth areas of the older regions of the Soviet Union sounds at times a little like the old Khrushchevian campaign jargon.[73] Perhaps most significant of all, the aftermath of the maize campaign has turned into something like an anti-maize campaign, with the crop being restricted in areas for which it is perfectly suitable.[74] But this sort of thing must be seen against the background of demographic and sociological factors which can change only at the slowest pace. Just about everyone wants to get away from the land, despite the great improvements in living standards. A survey done in village schools in the Crimea in December 1969 showed that more than 70 per cent wanted to go into urban employment and only 15 out of a total of 367 children interviewed wanted to go into agriculture.[75] Perhaps even more telling, of the 3·6 million mechanized agricultural workers trained in the period 1965–69, 79 per cent have entered employment outside agriculture. The increase in numbers of such workers employed in agriculture over the same period has been only 244,000.[76] It is perfectly clear that the basic problem here is the terrible lack of infrastructure, spiritual as well as material, the sheer *beskultur'e* ('culturelessness') of the village, rather than wage packets and pension rights.[77] But we can begin to perceive, through these bald figures, the reasons why the dilemma of control and initiative remains a cruel one, and why there have been instances of agricultural cadres complaining that the new policy of non-interference has been taken much too far.[78] It is quite clear that the continued development of intra-farm and farm autonomy and agro-industrial activity must present the brightest prospect for the future of Soviet agriculture, and that this development must depend on a consolidation of the principles of farm–non-farm relations that been established since 1964. One can only wait and see whether the long term can continue its ascendancy over the short term.

NOTES

1. See Nove, *An Economic History of the USSR*, Chapter 7.
2. See Carr, *The Bolshevik Revolution*, Vol. 2 Macmillan, London, 1952, pp. 151–176; *Socialism in One Country*, Vol. 1, Macmillan, London, 1958, pp. 230–233.
3. See J. F. Karcz, 'Thoughts on the grain problem', in *Soviet Studies*, April 1967, p. 411.
4. See M. Lewin, *Russian Peasants and Soviet Power*, Allen & Unwin, London, 1968, Chapter I.
5. M. Gor'kii, *O Russkom Krest'yanstve, Izdatel'stvo I. P. Ladyzhnikova*, Berlin, 1922, p. 43, quoted in A. Ulam, *Lenin and the Bolsheviks*, Secker & Warburg, London, 1966, p. 450.
6. See T. Kocharli, 'Nekotorye voprosy istorii kollektivizatsii sel'skogo khozyaistva v Azerbaidzhane', in *Voprosy Istorii KPSS*, 8/64.
7. Reprinted in English translation in J. Stalin, *Works*, Volume 12, Foreign Languages Publishing House, Moscow, 1955.
8. For figures on the uneven progress of collectivization, see Nove, *An Economic History of the USSR*, pp. 172 and 174.
9. See ibid., pp. 164–165.
10. See ibid., pp. 180–181.

11. Nove notes this in the case of potatoes for the postwar period. See ibid., p. 299.
12. See Nove, *The Soviet Economy* (2nd ed.), London, 1965, p. 59.
13. See Nove, 'Rural taxation in the USSR', in *Soviet Studies*, October 1953.
14. See J. F. Karcz, 'Soviet agriculture: a balance sheet', in Treml (ed.), *The Development of the Soviet Economy*.
15. J. Chapman, *op. cit.*
16. See Karcz, *op. cit.*
17. There is some controversy about Soviet war losses, estimates varying from 20 to 30 million.
18. See Strauss, *op. cit.*, pp. 108–109
19. See Nove, *The Soviet Economy* (3rd ed.), p. 57.
20. For an historical overview of the development of the state farm see C. R. Zoerb, 'From the promise of land and bread to the reality of the state farm', in ed. Treml, *The Development of the Soviet Economy*.
21. See Strauss, *op. cit.*, pp. 163–164.
22. See D. J. M. Hooson, *The Soviet Union*, University of London Press, 1966, pp. 203–204.
23. Calculated from *Narodnoe Khozyaistvo, SSSR v 1961 Godu*, Moscow, *Gosstatizdat*, 1962, pp. 292 and 300–301.
24. See L. Volin, 'Agricultural Policy of the Soviet Union' in Bornstein and Fusfeld (eds). *The Soviet Economy – A Book of Readings*, 3rd ed., Irwin, Homewood, Illinois, 1970.
25. See *Narodnoe Khozyaistvo SSSR v 1965 Godu, Statistike*, Moscow, 1966, p. 260.
26. There were 7·3 million tons of grain imports in 1964, compared with 0·1 million in 1938 and 0·2 million in 1960. See ibid., p. 672.
27. See D. Gale Johnson, 'Observations on the economy of the USSR', in *Journal of Political Economy*, June 1956, p. 206.
28. See Strauss, *op. cit.*, pp. 175–178; N. Jasny, *Khrushchev's Crop Policy*, Outram; Institute of Soviet and East European Studies, University of Glasgow, 1964, Chapter 2.
29. See Yu. Chernichenko, 'Tselinnaya doroga', in *Novyi Mir*, 1/64.
30. See A. Nove, 'Incentives for peasants and administrators', in

Was Stalin Really Necessary?, Allen & Unwin, London, 1964, pp. 186–190.

31. *Narodnoe Khozyaistvo v 1965 godu*, p. 536.
32. Strauss, *op. cit.*, p. 215
33. See K.-E. Wadekin, 'Private production in Soviet agriculture', in *Problems of Communism*, January–February 1968.
34. Nove, *An Economic History of the USSR*, p. 332.
35. See *Narodnoe Khozyaistvo v 1963 godu, Statistika*, Moscow, 1964, pp. 252–253.
36. See Nove, *An Economic History of the USSR*, pp. 364–365.
37. See speech by N. S. Khrushchev, published in *Pravda*, 6 March 1962, p. 6, quoted in Bergson, *The Economics of Soviet Planning*, Yale University Press, New Haven and London, pp. 221–222.
38. See L. Pistrak, *The Grand Tactician*, Thames and Hudson, London, 1961, Chapter 8.
39. See R. Conquest, *Russia After Khrushchev*, Pall Mall Press, London, 1965, pp. 102–103 and 122.
40. Grain imports averaged 3·5 million tons in the period 1965–71. See various editions of *Narodnoe Khozyaistvo SSSR*.
41. For a fuller discussion of these provisions see J. F. Karcz, 'The new Soviet agricultural programme', in *Soviet Studies*, October 1965; R. A. Clarke, 'Soviet agricultural reforms since Khrushchev', in *Soviet Studies*, October 1968.
42. See Clarke, *op. cit.*, pp. 160–161, n. 5.
43. See V. Isaev, 'Tverdaya, garantirovannaya', in *Ekonomicheskaya Gazeta*, 21/66, p. 9.
44. Sea V. Zhurikov, 'Luchshe ispolʹzovatʹ mery materialʹnogo pooshchreniya kolkhoznikov', in *Ekonomika Selʹskogo Khozyaistva*, 1/69, p. 6.
45. See Clarke, *op. cit.*, p. 160.
46. Ibid., p. 171.
47. A. Teryaeva, 'Neobkhodimyi trud i ego oplata v selʹskom khozyaistve', in *Voprosy Ekonomiki*, 5/72, p. 71.
48. L. Yagodin, 'Tovarishch iz raikoma', in *Ekonomicheskaya Gazeta*, 44/68, p. 26.
49. See Clarke, *op. cit.*, p. 164.
50. See Fainsod, *op. cit.*, pp. 538–539.
51. See D. Pospielovsky, 'The "link system" in Soviet agriculture', in *Soviet Studies*, April 1970, pp. 427–428.

52. See S. G. Kolesnevov, 'Ekonomicheskoe stimulirovanie i oplata truda v sel'skom khozyastve', in ed. V. F. Mel'nikov, *Ekonomika Sotsialisticheskogo Sel'skogo Khozyaistva v Sovremennykh Usloviyakh, Ekonomika*, Moscow, 1971, p. 233.

53. See I. Kopysov, 'krest'yanin i zemlya', in *Literaturnaya Gazeta*, 6/68, p. 10.

54. See Pospielovsky, *op. cit.*, pp. 425–426.

55. See A. Dergachev, 'Polevye soldaty nauki', in *Komsomol'skaya Pravda*, 22 August 1965, p. 2.

56. See, for example, V. Zhurikov, 'Organizatsiya, oplata i distsiplina truda', in *Ekonomika Sel'skogo Khozyaistva*, 8/70, pp. 38–40; N. T. Kozlov, 'Nauka khozyaistvovaniya', in *Ekonomicheskaya Gazeta*, 48/70, p. 18.

57. See Zhurikov, 'Organizatsiya, oplata . . .'.

58. G. A. Aksenenok, 'Pravo sel'skokhozyaistvennogo zemlepol'zovaniya v usloviyakh nauchno-tekhnicheskogo progressa', in *Sovetskoe Gosudarstvo i Pravo*, 7/71, pp. 31–32.

59. See L. Ivanov, 'Na tekh li dorogakh ishchem?', in *Literaturnaya Gazeta*, 25 September 1968, p. 10.

60. See K.-E. Wädekin, 'Manpower in Soviet agriculture – some post-Khrushchev developments and problems', in *Soviet Studies*, January 1969.

61. N. Gusev, 'Sel'skoe khozyaistvo v zavershayushchem godu pyatiletki', in *Ekonomika Sel'skogo Khozyaistva*, 3/70, p. 6.

62. M. Makeenko, 'Material' no-tekhnicheskaya osnova preodoleniya sushchestvennykh razlichii mezhdu gorodom i derevnei', in *Voprosy Ekonomiki*, 3/71, p. 71.

63. See N. Dergachev, 'O tsenakh na produktsiyu podsobnykh predpriyatii i promyslov kolkhozov i sovkhozov', in *Planovoe Khozyaistvo*, 2/70, pp. 75–78.

64. See K. Tidmarsh, 'Profit motive goes on trial in Russia,' in *The Times*, 21 June 1967.

65. See V. Kulikov, 'Nauchno-tekhnicheskii progress i sotsial'no-ekonomicheskie izmeneniya v derevne', in *Ekonomika Sel'skogo Khozyaistva*, 3/72, p. 40; Brezhnev himself advocated this kind of development at the 24th Congress of the CPSU; see I. Savvin, N. Zaderei, 'Agrarno-promyshlennye ob''edineniya i khozraschet', in *Kommunist Moldavii*, 3/72.

66. See Makeenko, *op. cit.*; A. Vydyborets, 'Zavod na sel' skoi ulitse', in *Komsomol'skaya Pravda*, 23 September 1969, p. 2;

V. Plyutinskii, 'Podsobnye predpriyatiya i promysly v kolkhozakh', in *Ekonomika Sel'skogo Khozyaistva*, 6/71.

67. For discussion of the problem of choosing subsidiary industrial activities with local labour conditions in mind, see G. Zelenskii and Ye. Voronin, 'Trudovye resursy v devyatoi pyatiletke', in *Planovoe Khozyaistvo*, 8/71, pp. 32–33.

68. Kulikov, *op. cit.*

69. F. Engels, *Anti-Dühring*, 3rd English edition, Foreign Language Publishing House, Moscow, 1962, pp. 400-409.

70. *Narodnoe Khozyaistvo v 1972 godu*, Moscow, 1973, p. 278; plan fulfilment report published in *Pravda*, 26 January 1974, p. 1.

71. See reports in *The Times*, 29 July 1974, p. 5; 7 October 1974, p. 1; 21 October 1974, p. 6.

72. See V. Darmodekhin, 'Medsestry na propolke', in *Izvestiya*, 4 July 1967, p. 3; O. Pavlov, 'Glavnoe deistvuyushchee litso', in *Izvestiya*, 16 August 1967, pp. 3-4; M. Gendel'man and A. Palii, 'Spetsializatsiya i ispol'zovanie zemel'nykh resursov', in *Ekonomika Sel'skogo Khozyaistva*, 10/71, p. 66.

73. For the original *postanovlenie* see *Pravda*, 3 April 1974, p. 1.

74. See A. Zadontsev *et al.*,'Vazhnyi rezerv zernovogo khozyaistva', in *Ekonomicheskaya Gazeta*, 10/71, p. 18; text of republican party and government decree in *Sovetskaya Moldaviya*, 29 April 1972, p. 1.

75. P. Yermishin, 'Shkol'nik vybiraet dorogu', in *Pravda*, 5 June 1970, p. 4.

76. A. Zalevskii, 'Polnee ispol'zovat' resursy truda', in *Ekonomika Sel'skogo Khozyaistva*, 4/72, p. 68.

77. See Ye. Dubrovin, 'Taini "gorodskogo prityazheniya"', in *Literaturnaya Gazeta*, 47/69, p. 10; note by I. M. Slepenkov, in *Komsomol'skaya Pravda*, 24 April 1970, p. 2.

78. See, for example, N. Kurapov *et al.*, 'Uspekhi ne prikhodyat sami', in *Ekonomicheskaya Gazeta*, 10/68, p. 31

CHAPTER EIGHT

Conclusions

The salient point which emerges from all the foregoing is that in studying the Soviet economic system we are studying a process, and a system of development. Much has been written about the Soviet 'model for development', and its 'exportability',[1] but the aim of this chapter, rather than to draw specific lessons, is simply to try to place the subject of our discussion more explicitly in an historical light, and to attempt some (hopefully) judicious generalization on the nature of planning systems.

It is terribly easy to be superior about the crudity of Soviet planning in the 1930s and 1940s. But when Naum Jasny, the old Menshevik planner, talks condescendingly about 'bacchanalian' planning,[2] he is really making the same point as Oscar Lange, when he describes the Soviet economy in the early stages as '*sui generis* a war economy'.[3] There never has been a war without hurrahs, certainly not a victorious one. Phrases and slogans such as 'there is no fortress the Bolsheviks cannot storm' (Stalinist, laudatory), 'the primacy of politics over economics' (ditto), 'voluntarism' (Khrushchevian, pejorative), 'shock work' (universal, laudatory) seem to present a common and very powerful suggestion that what happened in those heroic and bloody years somehow goes beyond the sphere of economics. In the narrow sense, this is obviously correct. No economist who is interested in things beyond the short-term and partial can afford to eschew the aid offered him by other disciplines, and indeed from sheer observation of the human condition. For all that, the phenomena of the 1930s and 1940s are not unamenable to economic analysis broader than the purely functional and basically static with which we largely contented ourselves in earlier chapters.

The setting of targets, success-indicators, taut planning, etc., are, as we have seen, all integral parts of the actual technology of plan construction and implementation. They are, however, equally part of the psychology of development. Bearing in mind the inevitable shortage of managerial personnel prevailing in the early days of industrialization, a shortage rendered the more severe by Stalin's policy of getting rid of the 'bourgeois specialists' of the 1920s;[4] bearing in mind the negligible level of education and almost total inexperience of machinery of the 'new' proletariat – typically a peasant hustled into industry by *orgnabor* – the general argument for a high degree of centralization was obvious. It was vitally necessary that specific tasks should be set, and set in terms readily understandable to the least sophisticated. A straightforward physical output target has a simplicity which no instruction or combination of instructions about work-rates, material-utilization norms, etc., can possibly have. But beyond this very general level of analysis we can see that output targets enjoy a unique and quite specific advantage. We noted in Chapter Four that aggregate growth targets are simply *sui generis* gross output targets, and that this presents problems to any planner who wants to work with a success-indicator system based on other criteria. The other side of the coin is of course that a gross output target gives a manager or worker an immediate and obvious basis on which to relate his own work to the performance of the economy as a whole. The identity of form of the aggregate growth target and the specific gross output target provides a means of direct socialization of the individual's effort to the collective goal which no other system of plan implementation can give. The fact that the socialization is often more apparent than real – viz. our earlier discussion of the success-indicator problem – is something that we shall have to return to later. At the present juncture we are emphasizing the psychological importance of the unique subjective identification which the gross output system gives. Soviet economic development, as it has proceeded, would have been inconceivable without the processions and the placards, and the processions and placards would have been poor enough affairs if profits and costs had been their only content and inspiration.

We should not of course fall into the trap of overstressing the historical importance of this aspect of incentives. Managerial behaviour is and has been, in general, very adequately predictable on the basis of reaction to material bonus schemes, and sheer terror may have been as important a galvanizing agent as any during the Stalin period, particularly in the late 1930s.[5] The attempt to combine high bonus levels with high levels of 'moral stimulation' for shopfloor workers – the Stakhanovite movement of the late 1930s – met with considerable resistance, and in one or two cases led to violence and murder.[6] The point is simply that we should be aware that moral stimulation may operate at a much cruder level than that of high-flown political idealism, and that the gross output system has certain unique advantages in this context.

Success-indicators are not only a part of the technology of planning, they are also uniquely tied in with the technology of production. Here again, if we place developments in historical perspective, certain crucial points emerge. As far as the quality/specification problem is concerned, serious distortions can be expected only with highly heterogeneous or highly complex products. Now of the four top priorities of the 1930s and 1940s – coal, steel, power and machinery – only the last fails to exhibit a marked degree of homogeneity and essential simplicity. There is no such thing as low-quality electricity. Power cannot be too thick, too thin, or too heavy. The case is not quite so clear-cut with coal and steel, but the basic point remains valid. A million tons of steel is a meaningful idea, even if the steel is rolled out too thick, or has too much carbon in it. A million tons of coal means something if there is too much brown and not enough coking coal. To put the matter into perspective, what does 'a million tons of computers' tell us about computer production? Obviously absolutely nothing, and 'a million tons of ladies' hats' tells us little enough about the state of the millinery sector.

There seems no reason to believe that the scope for bending cost constraints is any less great in basic than in secondary industrial activities. Indeed to try to argue that the system as it operated in the 1930s and 1940s was to any great extent less wasteful than it should have been is to miss one of the basic points about the whole Soviet approach to development, namely the complete lack of attention paid to micro-economizing as such. Whether it can be soundly argued as a general principle that micro-economizing is not very important in a development situation where labour and raw materials are not in short supply must remain a controversial issue. But no one denies the importance of micro-economizing in a developed industrial economy, and that is what the Soviet economy had become by the 1950s.

When we come to consider the question of innovation we can start off with the cautious statement that in some of the priority sectors of the Stalin period grass-roots resistance to innovation may have had little scope for operation. The technology of coal extraction has developed at a fairly slow rate, and at a given point in time is largely dictated by geographical and geological conditions. Technology choices in generating are obviously made at a level far above that of the shop floor. When we consider iron and steel and machinery, however, the generalization is difficult to sustain. On the other hand, if we move on to a higher level of generalization, we can perceive a very basic reason why innovation problems associated with the success-indicator regime may have been less serious at early stages of development. You can only get shop-floor resistance once there is a shop floor. A simple arithmetical fact about any country embarking on a programme of crash industrialization, especially one concerned to open up new areas, is that the relationship of the number of new plants under construction to the number of existing plants will be abnormally high over a period of years. The Soviet authorities obviously had no problems of grass-roots opposition to the introduction of the latest technology in the construction of the Urals-Kuznetsk Combine, which accounted for no less than 47 per cent of total investment expenditures in ferrous metallurgy in 1931![7]

None of these points about quality, specification and technology should be overstressed. A perusal of Berliner's classic study will assure the reader that all the familiar failings of the Soviet planning system were very obvious before the Second World War.[8] The point is simply that many of them must have been much less serious in quantitative terms than they later became.

We come now to the most difficult and controversial, though least neglected, aspect of Soviet economic development, namely the question of 'balance' and 'imbalance'. The ideology of the Soviet system is obviously on the side of balance – 'planned (proportional) development' and all that.[9] The practice, it has been argued, is much more in the direction of imbalance, and some

authors have tried to build up a fully fledged disequilibrium interpretation of the Soviet system. Thus, for example, Charles K.
Wilber:

> Growth tempos such as these (heavy industrial 1930s – D.A.D.)
> caused acute shortages and strains. The industrial bottlenecks which
> appeared then became the new targets. This is unbalanced growth
> with a vengeance. Much of the balanced growth versus unbalanced
> growth argument boils down to the question of where external
> economies are the greatest. One of the key questions in choosing
> investment criteria, in turn, hinges on how best to take advantage
> of external economies and avoid external diseconomies. Economic
> theorists usually argue that investment should be allocated in such
> a way that its social marginal product (SMP) is equal in all uses.
> While this is true as a formal statement it has no meaning unless the
> 'empty box' entitled SMP can be filled with some content. To date
> no one has done so. One advantage of the unbalanced growth
> strategy is that it provides a practical signal for reallocating invest-
> ment. When bottlenecks appear, the planners can be sure that the
> SMP of investment is not equal in all uses. The industries that are the
> bottlenecks will have a high SMP and thus should receive large
> investment allocations in the next period. In this sense the SMP
> will be equated in all uses through time, that is, in a dynamic sense.
> Thus the campaign method of unbalanced growth, though crude,
> does have a logic. It also entails a large risk of waste. If the bottle-
> necks are not quickly opened they can seriously retard economic
> growth.[10]

Now we must be quite clear what we are arguing about here. The
concept of bottleneck leads us logically on to an examination of
the Hirschmanian concept of 'linkage'.[11] But we must be very
careful about the relationship between this concept and the more
orthodox concept of externality. It is easy to slip from the Wilberian
dictum that 'while linkage is not the same thing as external
economies, it is probably a good indicator of where they lie',[12]
into a simple identification of linkage and externality. It may,
in fact, be worth pausing to refresh our memories about what
precisely is subsumed under the categories of externality and
linkage.

We distinguished in Chapter Five between production externalities, external economies of scale, and secondary agglomeration
economies. Let us look more closely at the last of these, taking the
classic case of the construction of a motorway. To the extent that

the profitability of petrol stations and cafeterias increases as a result of the new project, there will be a pecuniary spillover from transport users to the service sectors. But only if the construction of the motorway permits garages and restaurants to move on to a lower point on the cost curve or, more realistically, on to a lower cost technology altogether, is there any kind of externality present. Pure spillover effects have no place in cost-benefit calculations, but such effects may clearly have important macro-economic and distributional effects. The concept of linkage is basically just the concept of spillover, so that we can see from our example why, in practice, linkage and secondary agglomeration economies tend to be found together. The analytical distinction, however, remains perfectly clear. With linkage the emphasis is primarily on the creation of demand (backward linkages), the creation of new production possibilities (forward linkages), and more generally on the creation of tension, of bottlenecks. The question of costs, in other words the allocational aspect of the problem, is pushed into the background. The concept of externality, by contrast, places primary emphasis on just this aspect.

In what way, then, is pure linkage important in a centrally planned system, where there is no scope for market reaction to bottlenecks and the existence of spare capacity? Nove has argued that

> ... the entire *rationale* of the Soviet 'campaign' approach to economic planning rests upon ... the need to stimulate not only the executants but also the controllers ... Campaigns are among other things a means of goading the goaders, of mobilizing the controllers, of providing *success indicators* (my emphasis – D.A.D.) for officials at all levels.
>
> ... Hence the vital role of campaigns as controller mobilizers. Hence the value of bottlenecks as stimulators to effort.[13]

This passage graphically illustrates the need to get beyond the level of economic theory, even at its highest level of generalization, if we are fully to understand the problem in hand. But even at the level of straight economic analysis we see also that the distinction between plan construction and plan implementation, however useful for didactic purposes, cannot be made to bear too much weight. Let us begin to grapple with the problem by reminding ourselves of the basic difficulties facing the Soviet planners at the technical level of plan construction. Iterative techniques were too crude to yield even a moderately consistent plan, and in any case there were enormous problems of information, for both technological and system-induced reasons. The politico-economic leadership imposed certain constraints on the planners' quest for solutions to these problems. Consistency problems were never mollified by introducing slack. On the contrary, a strong emphasis was laid on tautness in plans. What this meant was that planned targets were often scaled up, hardly ever scaled down. If planned inputs into a given sector turned out to be inadequate, plans for the supplying sectors would normally simply be raised, irrespective of available information on production possibilities. The point is of course that available information was often imperfect in the extreme, so that it is quite incorrect to dismiss this kind of approach as merely 'impossible', as it obviously would be in a perfect input–output system. This in fact is basically how the Soviet bottlenecks were created. Planners would be presented with 'holes' in the plan which had to be filled one way or another, and the result for enterprise managers would eventually be targets which might bear little resemblance to what they had bargained for when they presented their *zayavki*, etc., but which would not necessarily be physically impossible. By emphasizing the essentially inter-sectoral character of this phenomenon, we show that it is a kind of Hirschmanian backward linkage effect.

One obvious riposte to this kind of argument would consist of a reminder that, after all, the system does induce concealment of capacity, and that no matter how much the planners may try to tighten, at least a few managers will get away with maintaining slack. This is true, but its importance is put in perspective if we study the results of studies of piecework systems in Western factories. It is widely accepted that piecework situations tend to be characterized by a form of capacity concealment known as the 'bogey', or unofficial quota. Nevertheless a National Board for Prices and Incomes report noted that 'there was wide agreement in the general evidence we received that the most usual reason for installing PBR (Payment By Results – D.A.D.) had been to raise output, and that it had been effective in doing so'.[14] Now this conclusion is based on no assumption of a high degree of tautness in target-setting. In fact, the evidence is quite conclusive that tautness is simply not acceptable in a Western factory, and tends simply to result in a form of go-slow called 'goldbricking'.[15] It is quite clear, however, that any such tactics were simply not on for a Soviet manager or worker who valued his freedom and his life in the Stalin period. The negative effect on output of capacity concealment must, therefore, have been considerably more than cancelled out by the combined positive effect of the output indicator/bonus system and taut planning.

A more serious problem arising with the argument is that of dislocation, or potential dislocation. As Wilber says, 'If the bottlenecks are not quickly opened they can seriously retard economic growth.' What happens if non-fulfilment of a key target does become imminent? Clearly the crucial consideration here is the relationship between key and non-key targets. One simple point: without consideration of possible resource movements as such, an approach which places primary emphasis on targets for intermediate rather than final goods reduces the potential danger of dislocation very considerably. If there is a shortfall, say, in the production of one of the inputs into steel, the catastrophe is lightened by the secondary importance attached to reverberations beyond the stage of steel production itself.[16] Much more important, however, it is extremely unlikely that in such a case the shortfall would be allowed to affect the production level of steel. This brings us back to the famous priority principle, whose operation we outlined in Chapter Two.

According to the priority principle, if there is a danger that a target in a priority sector might be missed, resources are simply physically shifted out of non-priority sectors in order to ensure fulfilment of the key targets. Shortfalls in plan fulfilment in non-priority sectors (i.e. principally light industry) in the 1930s sometimes reached 25 per cent, and this is as crucial a feature of the picture as the 'impossible' acheivements of the top-priority sectors.[17]

Now the priority principle has a number of important aspects. An obvious one is that it necessarily tends to produce a lower consumption ratio than appears in the initial plan – goods that are never produced cannot be consumed. In other words, we have a kind of forced saving, and it is this that the inflation of the middle and late 1930s may have been designed to conceal.[18] For present purposes, however, the important point is that in a situation where there are just a few priority and a large number of non-priority sectors, and as long as resources are reasonably mobile between sectors, the danger of any kind of dislocation that is actually considered to be serious must be pretty well minimized. Looking at it from a more formal point of view, the whole problem of consistency is simplified to such an extent as almost to disappear from view.

One subsidiary conclusion which flows from the foregoing is that forward linkage has been of much less importance than backward linkage in the Soviet context. The higher the priority on steel *per se*, the less pressure would there be to probe deeply into new production possibilities opened up by the higher level of steel production, except of course in the other top-priority sectors. The nature of the system has in fact, as we have seen, tended to channel any surplus stocks into the ramifications of the *tolkach* system; in other words, into another of the mechanisms whereby the dislocatory dangers of bottlenecks have been minimized.

With linkage *per se* out of the way, we can return to a consideration of externalities *per se*. We saw in Chapter Five how insensitive the system of plan implementation has been to production externalities, and how difficult it has been for the central authorities to correct this. As far as secondary agglomeration economies are concerned, we must repeat that the predominance of the gross output success-indicator has tended to militate against cost-consciousness in general. The central planners, on the other hand, have often neglected close consideration of the effects of big projects on the parameters of potential customers for the same reason that they have not been primarily interested in forward linkages. With potential suppliers, the case is more difficult. Planners have been concerned with backward linkages, so they have been concerned to maximize outputs of inputs for key enterprises. Certainly short-run output maximization may correspond very little to optimal production conditions. Nevertheless the preoccupation with scale, whatever its basis, must have brought some economies, and these economies may in some cases have had a significant cumulative effect beyond the key project itself – scale, in effect, breeding scale. Let us take, for example, the Bratsk hydro-electric scheme. Here capacity was constructed ahead of demand to an extent hardly justifiable by any reference to growth tactics,[19] especially in a system where forward linkage cannot be expected to be a very powerful force. On the other hand, electricity is not a commodity that can be transported farther than a few thousand kilometres, and this is a real limitation when one is working on the scale of Siberia. Willy-nilly, some local use for the power had to be found. The wood-cellulose, ore-concentrating and aluminium plants which were eventually completed, and which became the principal users of Bratsk power, fulfilled this need, and could operate on a scale which would not have been possible without Bratsk (at least until the Krasnoyarsk station was completed), irrespective of any consideration of the cost of electricity. In any case, the electricity *is* very cheap.

But we are getting very close to external economies of scale here. As the Eastern Siberian industrial zone builds up all the usual transport and amenities economies will accrue. (It would be unwise too rashly to predict the building up of a pool of skilled labour in Eastern Siberia! See discussion in Chapter Six.) But the development of a region must start somewhere. A cheap source of energy is as good a place as any, though in the Urals and West Siberia it was cheap coal and iron ore. The general point, and it is a very important point, is that the Soviet system, for all its crudity – perhaps because of its crudity, which may have sharpened perception of big things through so completely blurring perception of small – has been well adapted to the exploitation of external economies of scale through the opening up of new regions.

The importance of this aspect of Soviet planning can be underlined by looking at the pattern of development in Central Asia, an area with, at least initially, few spectacular known fuel and mineral resources and a totally undeveloped urban/industrial infrastructure. We have already seen that the region has suffered severely from ministerial tendencies to ignore production diseconomies, and to autarky in supply patterns. The detailed pattern of industrial location in the region does, in fact, present a hodge-podge such as has bewildered Western economists and enraged their colleagues from Central Asia.[20] Be that as it may, comprehensive control over major sectoral proportions plus the command principle have enabled the Soviet authorities to build up the Central Asian region in a fairly well-rounded way so that external economies of scale have been reaped on a high, if by no means maximal, level. Initial heavy emphasis on development of agriculture – principally cotton – was followed after the Second World War by intensive development of ginning, cottonseed oil capacity, etc. The development of cotton-orientated engineering was an aspect of strategy only partially implemented, for reasons already discussed. But by the 1950s the Central Asian economy presented a sufficiently integrated profile to permit the exploitation of considerable transport economies, as well as secondary agglomeration effects, let the ministries do what they might. Equally important, the whole development effort in Central Asia was supported throughout by a sustained programme of building up an educational and social infrastructure which, whatever its cultural side-effects, succeeded in producing a disciplined and, on the whole, adequately trained labour force.[21]

It would be unrealistic to pretend that the Soviet record on transport externalities has been in general all that good. In more complex cases than Central Asia and Siberia, e.g. in the Central European areas themselves, ministerial penchants may quite possibly have won the day. More consistently exploited has been the 'human capital' aspect of this type of externality. The scope for dovetailing educational and industrial programmes, backed up by ideological push, has aided the building up of skilled cadres in very quick time (Siberia and the Far East always excepted!). In Central Asia the socializing programme has worked at the most general level. In other areas the emphasis has been much more on particular sectors of industry. The development of Volga oil, for example, was not hindered by cadre problems in the way that the development of vehicle production in Scotland has been.[22] On the other hand, inherited advantages within the same broad category have not been dissipated. Thus the 200-year-old tradition of the Moscow region has remained the basis of the textile industry, despite protests from Central Asian economists who would like to see a greater concentration of all stages of cotton processing in the primary producing area itself.[23]

The foregoing should not be seen as the presentation of a comprehensive, interlocking Soviet strategy for development. Rather should it be seen as a listing of advantages which may have accrued to the Soviet system in the development period, together with some more or less *a priori* suggestions tending to the notion that some characteristic deficiencies may have been less serious in the earlier than in the later period. We must always bear in mind, of course, the tremendous importance of the simple fact of an enormously high investment rate as a factor in Soviet economic performance. The point is, however, that this high investment rate was made effective in a way which does not always apply to high investment rates in developmental situations.[24] It is perhaps significant that one of the first danger signals that the times might be out of joint was a serious drop in the marginal efficiency of capital. This was accompanied by the problem of rising stocks of unsaleable goods, and eventually by a serious drop in the rate of growth itself. The *a priori* arguments presenting themselves as an explanation of these phenomena run as follows:

1. With increased heterogeneity and/or technical complexity of goods, the quality/specification aspect of the success-indicator problem became more and more serious.

2. With the increasing complexity of inter-sectoral relationships within the economy the negative aspects of disequilibrium in planned production flows and crudeness in approaches to the solution of such disequilibria became increasingly important.

3. To make matters worse, the escalation of priorities which occurred in the early 1950s, with greater emphasis on light industry, agriculture, chemicals, etc., weakened the strength of the priority principle as a 'fail-safe' in cases of inter-sectoral and inter-product disequilibrium.

4. With the increasing sophistication of the workforce, both managerial and shop-floor, certain advantages of a high degree of centralization and a highly simplified success-indicator system ceased to be of major importance.

5. With the ever-increasing pace of technical progress on a world scale, and with the transition of the Soviet economy to a high-technology basis, the importance of speedy implementation of foreign and domestic innovations became increasingly important.

But it would be a gross oversimplification to see the problems of the maturing Soviet economy purely in terms of the need to replace an outmoded model with something more apposite to the technical realities of the period. Equally important, as a high level of national income per head was achieved, a growing area of choice of basic aims began to present itself. The basic decision facing the Soviet leadership is not just 'how best do we keep up growth rates and make sure that presentable goods are produced', but 'how important is the maintenance of a high rate of growth, if this cannot be guaranteed simultaneously with the maintenance of high standards of quality of goods and services?' In practice, of course, the dilemma becomes much more complex, and it is perhaps worth listing the principal considerations which may complicate the picture.

(a) As the economy approaches an advanced level of development, there may be a 'natural' tendency for growth rates to decline, for arithmetical if for no other reasons.[25]

(b) Maintenance of the command system may be seen as a necessary condition of the maintenance of defence priorities.

(c) Even if defence priorities could be maintained in the long run, the general geopolitical and strategic implications of a longish period of transition and readjustment, such as would inevitably accompany any radical economic reform, might be held to be unacceptable.

(d) The Party *apparat* may be sufficiently strong as a vested interest to prevent any reforms so radical as to make redundant the 'trouble-shooting' role of the *apparat*, even if such a reform were favoured by the central Party leadership.[26]

(e) The managerial establishment, or one or more of its components – planning personnel, ministerial workers, enterprise managers – could emerge as a strong pressure group for some kind of decentralizing reform.[27]

(f) The 'Human Rights Movement' could precipitate a situation of general flux, such as would be conducive to a rethinking of all aspects of national life, including economic affairs.[28]

(g) A radical improvement in living standards may be necessary to prevent the emergence of mass discontent in the population at large, quite apart from appearing desirable *per se* to the leadership.

(h) A growing level of economic intercourse with the rest of the world may be a necessary condition of ensuring that technology is kept up to scratch. The more 'open' the Soviet economy becomes, however, the more necessary it will be to evolve some way of translating domestic economic realities into world trading prices – and that almost certainly means some degree of marketization.

These, then, are the broad politico-economic constraints which affect Soviet policy alternatives. But we must in addition bear in mind a number of more or less technical economic points which emerged from the discussion in Chapters Two to Four.

THE SOVIET ECONOMY

(i) Output targets are peculiarly growth orientated, and no other indicator or set of indicators can be expected, under real conditions, to produce anything more than a fairly strong probability that a given rate of growth will be approximated.

(ii) The success-indicator problem can never be wholly obviated with any set of success-indicators without some element of marketization, i.e. some degree of freedom of contract and/or price formation.

(iii) It may be possible to combine command and market elements intra-sectorally, but a necessary, if not sufficient, condition of a successful marriage would be the introduction of a significant degree of 'official' slack into the system, with the abandonment of ratchet planning, which would probably be possible only on the basis of some general decentralization.

(iv) Any policy which attempts to solve problems through more detailed and effective control is likely to fail for the same reasons that similar policies have failed in the past, but could in any case be completely disastrous, since it is through *de facto* decentralization, often involving the infringement of regulations, and actions which must be considered *ceteris paribus* undesirable, that the supply system is kept going.

(v) As the importance of regular supplies of high-quality goods becomes increasingly important within the industrial sphere itself, so the growth/quality dilemma becomes increasingly unreal.

(vi) The possibilities of computer technology in practice strengthen the rationalized decentralization rather than the perfect computation argument.

The gist of all this might appear to be that the Soviet authorities are faced with enormous, well-nigh insoluble problems, and are hemmed in on every side by obstacles to significant change. The situation is not, of course, nearly as bad as that. The point is simply that economic policy in the Soviet Union is as complex a matter, and subject to as many constraints, as it is elsewhere in the world. Some of the constraints are not, or at least not yet, of any great importance. There is no real evidence of the emergence of a strong managerial socio-political identity, nor is there any evidence to suggest that political dissidents are likely to achieve mass support in the near future. The post-1965 planning system continues to produce reasonable rates of growth, and some trend towards the improved quality of goods. It is quite possible that the authorities remain principally concerned with the former – that indeed the origin of the reform lay in the low rates of growth, rather than the poor-quality goods, of the early 1960s. If so, the modesty of the changes in the aspects of the system which affect quality and specification have not as yet proved to be insuperable obstacles to continued economic growth at a very respectable rate. The *a priori* case that this situation cannot continue indefinitely is a very strong one, but clearly time is still some way from running out.

The question of increasing living standards may become crucial rather earlier. The 1971–75 five-year plan gives the planned rate of increase for means of consumption as 44–48%, and the planned rate for means of production as 41–45%. In other words, the time-honoured primacy of Department A has well and truly gone. These figures tell us nothing conclusive about consumption and investment, because they are based on gross, not value-added statistics, and Department A includes intermediate as well as investment goods. On the assumption, however, that no significant changes in degrees of vertical integration are occurring, and taking defence and governmental expenditures as given, they must imply an increase in the rate of consumption, at the expense of the rate of investment. We must now remind ourselves of the problems of the investment sector, as discussed in Chapter Five. The problem of excessive gestation periods, rising costs, etc. – in other words the problem of the general level of efficiency in the sector – have shown no signs of being alleviated by the reform. Indeed the new emphasis on cost constraints may be simply exacerbating the problem of gestation periods by making it more difficult to keep supply flows going by unofficial means. Now it is simple arithmetic that if a drop in the investment rate is not to result in a slowdown in economic growth, it must be made up for by an increase in the effectiveness of new investment. Obviously the technology to be embodied in the new investment is an important variable here, and that in itself is a problem for the Soviet system. But with the most advanced technology in the world, if the actual process of implementing plans remains clumsy and costly, then there can be no effective transition from extensive to intensive development. It is surely for this reason that for the last year of the 1971–75 five-year plan the old priority for means of production was re-established.[30]

Lastly, and perhaps most important, how serious are the political and strategic barriers to radical change? The party apparatus is certainly a most powerful group. It played an important part in the strengthening of Khrushchev's position in 1957, and in his eventual removal in 1964. On the other hand, we have no evidence from the Soviet Union itself of the apparatus setting itself up in opposition to the party leadership as a whole, as distinct from taking sides in an intra-leadership struggle. It is, of course, possible to conceive of a situation where the policy orientation of a weak leadership with few policy ideas of its own might be effectively dictated by the apparatus, but this would appear to remain, for the moment, hypothetical. The defence lobby is certainly important, but there has never been a case in Soviet history where the military has opposed the party leadership and won. We should, then, perhaps be more concerned about the views of the leadership itself about strategic needs than about the defence establishment as a socio-political grouping.

When we look at the command system from a purely defence point of view, the balance of advantages and disadvantages changes radically. As has been forcefully shown in a recent piece of research, the Soviet authorities have no difficulty in keeping up the level of quality and technology in a sector which is directly and continuously under central surveillance.[31] In addition the tremendous importance of the priority principle in any defence set-up is obvious, and a fully fledged priority system is inconceivable without the command principle. It is clear from American experience that it is possible to integrate a large defence establishment into a market economy, but problems of transition to such a 'mixed' system would obviously be very considerable. Transition to the other kind of mixed system – where command and market principles coexist within sectors – might be less traumatic, and there would be no need to abandon the priority principle. Growth maximization, however, would have to go (if it has not already gone), though it would still be possible to guarantee a given rate of growth within a few percentage points. Equally important, careful experiment would have to be carried on to ascertain precisely how such a mixture would work out in practice – there is little enough past experience to go on.

It would be wrong, then, to see the Soviet leadership as caught in a cleft stick. What is absolutely clear is that further economic reform is necessary. What is equally clear is that meaningful economic reform must involve the abandonment of growth maximization, though not necessarily of growth-consciousness. Lastly, reform must be orientated to the specific needs of the Soviet Union – external and internal, political and strategic, as well as narrowly economic. But there is no reason to believe that, with the aid of judicious experimentation, practicable and realistic solutions may not be found.

NOTES

1. See, for example, A. Nove and J. A. Newth, *The Soviet Middle East. A Communist Model for Development?* Allen & Unwins, London, 1967; C. K. Wilber, *The Soviet Model and Underdeveloped Countries*, University of North Carolina Press, Chapel Hill, 1969.
2. N. Jasny, *Soviet Industrialization 1928–52*, Chicago University Press, 1961, p. 73.
4. O. Lange, 'Role of planning in Socialist economy', in ed., O. Lange, *Problems of Political Economy of Socialism*, People's Publishing House, New Delhi, 1962, p. 18.
4. For a graphic description of a typical 'red executive' of the early 1930s, see J. Scott, *Behind the Urals*, Secker & Warburg, London, 1943, pp. 137–143.
5. See, for example, V. Kravchenko, *I Chose Freedom*, Robert Hale, London, 1947.
6. See ed. Conquest, *Industrial Workers in the USSR*, p. 79.
7. Holzman, *op. cit.*, p. 382, quoting Ya. Ioffe, 'Uralo-Kuznetskii kombinat v kontrol'nykh tsifrakh 1931 goda', in *Puti Industrializatsii*, 3–4/31, p. 29.
8. Berliner, *Factory and Manager in the USSR*, Harvard University Press, Cambridge, Mass., 1957.
9. See Nove, *The Soviet Economy* (3rd ed.), p. 321.
10. Wilber, *op. cit.*, pp. 87–88.
11. See A. Hirschman, *The Strategy of Economic Development*, Yale University Press, New Haven, 1958.
12. Wilber, *op. cit.*, p. 90.
13. Nove, *The Soviet Economy* (3rd ed.), p. 308.

14. National Board for Prices and Incomes, Report No. 65, *Payment by Results Systems*, London, 1968, Cmnd. 3627, p. 20.
15. See D. Roy, 'Quota restriction and goldbricking', in ed. Lupton, *op. cit.*
16. This point corresponds interestingly with the theoretical point that a system which starts the iterative process from intermediate goods will have a better approximation to consistency after one iteration than if it had started from final goods. See J. M. Montias, 'Planning with material balances in Soviet-type economies', in *American Economic Review*, December 1959, p. 968.
17. See H. Hunter, 'Priorities and shortfalls in prewar Soviet planning', in ed. J. Degras and A. Nove, *Soviet Planning. Essays in Honour of Naum Jasny*, Blackwell, Oxford, 1964.
18. See Schwarz, *op. cit.*, pp. 133–145 and 152–163.
19. E. Gorbunov, B. Orlov, 'O narodnokhozyaistvennoi effektivnosti razvitiya promyshlennosti v Sibiri', in *Voprosy Ekonomiki*, 8/66, pp. 55–56.
20. See, for example, Sh. N. Zakirov, *Voprosy Razvitiya i Razmeshcheniya Promyshlennosti Uzbekistana*, NaukaUzSSR, Tashkent 1965.
21. See Wilber, *op. cit.*, Chapter 8.
22. See A. A. Trofimuk, *Uralo-Povolzh'e – Novaya Neftyanaya Baza SSSR, Gostoptekhizdat*, Moscow, 1957.
23. See, for example, S. V. Vladimirov, 'Legkaya promyshlennost'', in ed. I. K. Narzikulov, *Problemy Razvitiya i Razmeshcheniya Proizvoditel'nykh Sil Tadzhikskoi SSR*, Donish, Dushanbe, 1967, pp. 105–107.
24. Argentina, with an average non-residential gross fixed investment rate of 14·3 per cent in the period 1950–66 showed a rate of growth of gross domestic product of 3·0 per cent in the period 1950–68. See A. Maddison, *Economic Progress and Policy in Developing Countries*, Allen & Unwin, London, 1970, pp. 29 and 37.
25. The arithmetical argument rests on the simple fact that at early stages of development a large percentage increase may represent an extremely modest advance in absolute terms. For discussion of other factors see A. Gerschenkron, *Economic Backwardness in Historical Perspective*, Harvard University Press, Cambridge, Mass., 1966, pp. 261–264.

26. For a most interesting discussion of the *apparatchik* vested interest problem in the case of the Czechoslovak reforms of 1966–68, see L. Urbanek, 'Some difficulties in implementing the economic reforms in Czechoslovakia', in *Soviet Studies*, April 1968. Note, however, that we cannot in the Czechoslovak case speak of a Party leadership wholly united on basic policy.

27. For a discussion of this issue, see J. Azrael, *Managerial Power and Soviet Politics*, Harvard University Press, Cambridge, Mass., 1966.

28. For interesting material on political dissent in the Soviet Union, see ed. P. Reddaway, *Uncensored Russia*, Capes, London, 1972; *A Chronicle of Current Events* (periodical), Amnesty International Publications; *A Chronicle of Human Rights in the USSR* (periodical), Khronika Press, New York.

29. See report of speech by A. N. Kosygin, in *Pravda*, 11 April 1971, p. 2.

30. See statement on annual plan for 1975 published in *Pravda*, 21 December 1974, p. 1.

31. See R. W. Cambell, 'Management spillovers from Soviet space and military programmes', in *Soviet Studies*, April 1972.

Glossary

apparatchik professional Communist Party apparatus man
attestat zrelosti certificate of fitness
babushka grandmother, old woman
firma firm
glavk main administration, principal sub-division of ministry
Gosarbitrazh State Arbitration
Gosbank State Bank
Gosplan State Planning Commission
Gossnab State Committee for Supply
Gosstroi State Committee for Construction
Gosudarstvennaya priemochnaya kommissiya State Operationalization Commission
khozraschet 'economic accounting'
kolkhoz collective farm
kolkhoznik collective farm worker
kombinat combine
Komsomol Communist Youth League
kontrol' inspection
kontrol'nye tsifry 'control figures'
krai province
mestnichestvo localism
MTS machine-tractor station
naryad materials allocation order
NOT – nauchnaya organizatsiya truda scientific organization of labour
ob''edinenie association
obkom provincial party committee
oblast province
orgnabor organized recruitment
predpriyatie enterprise
pribyl' profit
prodrazverstka compulsory procurement

proektnaya organizatsiya design organization
proektnoe zadanie design assignment
profsoyuzy trade unions
pryamye svyazi 'direct links'
raion district
raspylenie sredstv 'spreading' or 'dispersion' of investment resources
rentabel'nost rate of profit
RTS repair-technical station
shturmovshchina 'storming'
sotsialisticheskoe sorevnovanie socialist competition
sovkhoz state farm
sovnarkhoz regional economic council
Stroibank Construction Bank
tekuchest' excessive labour mobility
tekhnicheskii proekt technical design
territorial'no-proizvodstvennoe upravlenie territorial-production administration
titul'nyi spisok 'title list'
tolkach 'pusher'
trest trust
trudoden' conventional work day
trudoustroistvo labour placement
upolnomochennyi plenipotentiary
valovaya produktsiya gross output
vedomstvennost' departmentalism
VUZ – vyhesse uchebnoe zavedenie higher educational institution
vypusknik graduate
zayavka indent for material supply
zveno 'link'

Name Index

Andreev, A. A. 138

Berliner, J. 150
Brezhnev, L. I. 58, 136
Brown, E. C. 113, 114

Ellman, M. 26, 35
Engels, F. 141

Grant, N. 102

Hirschman, A. 151

Jasny, N. 147

Kaganovich, L. 54
Kantorovich, L. 34
Karcz, J. 125
Khrushchev, N. S. 54, 55, 56, 58, 62, 84, 103, 128–136, 162
Konovalova, F. 100
Kosygin, A. N. 58, 59, 136

Lange, O. 147
Lenin, V. I. 2

Leontief, W. 29
Levine, H. 26
Liberman, E. 57, 58

Malenkov, G. 54
Matskevich, V. V. 141
Molotov, V. M. 54

Nemchinov, V. S. 34, 57
Nove, A. 124, 152
Novozhilov, V. V. 34

Podgornyi, N. V. 58, 136
Polyanskii, D. S. 141

Richman, B. 39

Stalin, I. V. 3, 33, 54, 101, 124, 126
Stolypin, P. 2, 122
Strauss, E. 131

Wilber, C. K. 151, 154
Witte, S. 2

Yagodin, L. 137

Subject Index

[171]

Input-output 28–30
Inspection 14
'Intra-project title list,' *see Vnutri-
postroechnyi titul'nyi spisok*

Kandidat 105
Khozraschet 59, 137–138
Khozyaistvennyi sposob 79
Kindergartens 115–116
Kolkhoz 3, 12, 13, 102, 126–131, 136–
137
Kolkhoz market 12, 22, n.17, 106,
126–127
Kolkhozniki 12, 102, 127, 131, 137,
140
Kombinat 11
Komsomol 102, 108, 119 n.25
Kontrol', *see* Inspection
Kontrol'nye tsifry 27

Labour camps 101
Labour placement 111–113
Labour reserve schools 99
Limits 76–78
Linear programming 30, 34
Link, *see Zveno*
Linkage 151–152, 155
Localism 54–56
Location, theory of 83

Maize campaign 132, 141
Marxian 2, 15, 16
Material balances 25–27, 30
Material incentives 38–41, 56, 58,
60, 70–71, 148–149, 153–154
Mestnichestvo, *see* Localism
Micawber principle 40, 44, 46
Ministry 11, 20, 28, 47, 54, 58, 59, 64–
65, 71, 77–80, 82, 86–89 91–92,
109, 156
Monetary control 13–14
Moral incentives 38–39, 45, 60, 65,
113–114, 148–149
MTS 129

Naryad 50
Nationalisation 2
NEP 2

NKVD 101
NOT 106, 120 n.55

Ob"edinenie 11, 12, 59, 65, 71, 140
Orgnabor 101–102, 108, 111

Passport 100–101
Permafrost 4–5, 8–9
Plenipotentiary, *see Upolnomochennyi*
Podryadni sposob 79
Police registration 100–101
Polytechnicization 103–104
Population 4, 6–7
Power resources 4
Prices 5, 10, 12, 15, 16, 35, 41–42,
45, 58, 60, 67, 68, 124, 126,
128–130, 136
Priority, priority principle 3, 28, 38,
154–155, 158, 162
Private plot 12, 124–127, 132
Procurement 2, 4, 12, 123, 134
Proektnaya organizatsiya, *see* Design
organisation
Proektnoe zadanie, *see* Design assign-
ment
Professional'no-tekhnicheskie uchilishcha,
see Vocational-technical schools
Pusher, *see Tolkach*

Rabochie chertezhi, see Working draw-
ings
Raspylenie sredstv 82
Ratchet principle 40, 44, 46, 70, 71
Raw material deposits 4, 8–9
'Reconstruction and expansion' 77,
86
Rent 16, 43, 60, 90, 92
Republican planning authorities 77–
78
Research and development, *see* In-
novation
RTS 129

Secondary specialised schools 104
Sel'khoztekhnika 131
Shchekino experiment 112–113, 117
Shturmovshchina 43–44, 63–64, 114–
115